Keto Vegan

Lose Weight Fast and Healthy

By

Aaron Smith

Table of Contents

Introduction

The ketogenic diet is a high-fat and very low-carb diet that has many health benefits for its users. It's great for weight-loss and other aspects of our wellbeing. The keto diet shares lots of similarities with the Atkins Diet and several other low-carb diets.

It has to do with the drastic reduction of the individual's carbohydrate intake and the replacement of it with fat. Due to this reduction of carbs, the body goes into a metabolic state known as ketosis. Whenever this happens, the body becomes quite efficient at burning the excess fat to produce energy. This particular diet causes a massive decrease in insulin levels and blood sugar, which also has multiple health benefits. The ketogenic diet has different types and forms of it; amongst which the keto-vegan diet is part of them.

The "keto" in the ketogenic diet is derived from the fact it permits the body to produce tiny molecules of fuel known as "ketones." It's an alternative source of fuel that's only used when there's a short supply of glucose.

Ketones are produced when high levels of fats are consumed while the carbs are reduced immensely. The liver uses the fats to produce ketones, which then serve as energy for the various organs in the body –especially the brain. It's great when you want to lose weight or gain other beneficial aspects. Fewer hunger pangs and a steady energy supply allows the body to stay focused and alert.

While the fastest way to achieve ketosis is by fasting (not eating anything), no one can fast forever; hence, the need for the high-fat-consumption option. The ketogenic diet has all the benefits that come with fasting – that is without having to fast.

Other forms of the keto diet include;

- Targeted Ketogenic Diet: Which involves consuming a day's worth of carbohydrates in a pre-exercise meal.
- Cyclic Ketogenic Diet: It has to do with periods of carb-loading, and is also known as keto cycling.
- Restricted Ketogenic Diet: It reduces calorie and carb intake with the general idea of fighting cancer (even though it hasn't been proven by medical research yet)
- High-Protein Ketogenic Diet: It involves an increased percentage of calories that come from proteinic foods.

Throughout the world, the vegetarian and vegan lifestyle has been regarded as one of the healthiest diets humans could ever adopt. Several studies conducted show how vegans reduce their likelihood of developing heart disease or diabetes based on the foods they eat. Regardless of how excellent the diet is, it doesn't necessarily mean it's the best option for everyone.

Despite how popular the ketogenic diet is right now; a lot of people still misunderstand its concept. They feel it's merely a carnivore-style diet that naturally excludes vegans. Fortunately, this isn't the case. There are lots of ways to incorporate the vegan lifestyle into the keto diet.

promoting weight loss, improving blood sugar and triglyceride levels, while reducing the severity of various diseases (Alzheimer's, epilepsy, diabetes, obesity, etc.).

Just as with everything else in life, there's always a downside to everything.

The ketogenic diet is saddled with multiple health concerns as well as environmental ones too. The major problem for some individuals stems from the source of animal products like meat and milk. Lots of people frown upon the way the animals are reared and slaughtered.

While it's possible to stick to either the ketogenic or the vegan diet separately, merging the two of them to form one plan helps improve health drastically. That's where the keto-vegan diet comes in handy.

Chapter One

Where the Keto-Vegan Diet was born

The original ketogenic diet first started making waves in the 1920s where it began as a form of treatment for pediatric epilepsy. It served as a therapeutic diet which provided a reasonable amount of protein for body growth and repair, and enough calories needed to maintain the right weight for age and height.

The treatment was used widely by different institutions before its popularity began fading with the introduction of more effective anticonvulsant medications.

The ketogenic diet started as a mainstream dietary therapy designed to replicate the success of the non-mainstream use of fasting to cure epileptic patients while removing the limitations that surrounded it.

Due to the emergence of anticonvulsant drugs, the diet once making waves in the 1920s and '30s started fading away slowly; although it never actually went away. While the medication made it possible for most individuals to control their seizures successfully, about 20-30% of them failed to do so – even when they tried different drugs. This group of people (mostly children) that the medication couldn't work for relied on the ketogenic diet to ease their seizures.

Ancient Greek Origins

Thousands of years ago, the Greeks believed epilepsy was caused by spiritual possession. They dubbed it the "Sacred Disease" because it was so powerful it couldn't be cured. About a hundred years later, Hippocrates, the Father of Medicine, came along and discredited the whole thing.

He showed the Greeks the disease wasn't unlike any other ones and didn't have a supernatural cause; rather a natural one which couldn't be cured back then due to man's inexperience.

Hippocrates' mindset change went on to be dubbed as one of the most significant medical breakthroughs in history. He gave the Greeks the longed for cure when he prescribed complete abstinence from food and drink for a patient who got cured shortly afterward.

Hippocrates had discovered the power of ketones and how they fuel the body when food runs short. His treatment marked the first recorded use of therapeutic ketosis.

France

In 1911, the first modern scientific study using fasting as a cure was conducted in France. Initially, they'd been making use of Potassium Bromide to treat epileptic patients, but it ended up slowing their mental capabilities.

The doctors believed epilepsy was a result of masturbation, and Bromide served as a powerful sedative that zapped individuals of any sexual excitement. The medication worked in curing the epilepsy, but it also zapped the patients of every other feeling. It made them lifeless and sick.

Based on the setbacks experienced with Bromide, the doctors went back to the option of fasting. They started with twenty patients and made them follow a vegetarian food plan with low-calories, combined with fasting. Two of them showed major improvements to their health, even though several others couldn't keep up with the dietary restrictions.

The doctors found that the diet improved their patients' mental capabilities when compared to the effects gotten with the usage of the Potassium Bromide.

The United States

In the early 20th Century, American fitness guru and 'physical cultist,' Bernarr McFadden popularized Keto and fasting as a means of restoring health. His theory was that digesting of food required tons of energy, and if there weren't anything to digest, our body would use the conserved energy in restoring our health.

Bernarr claimed that every ailment could be cured by fasting, from epilepsy to asthma. Although, he didn't have any credentials to back up his claims; all he had was his experience.

Several years later, Dr. Hugh Conklin set up a homeopathic practice in the Midwest, where he offered therapy for epileptic patients through fasting. He proposed that the seizures were caused by a toxin secreted in the intestines and recommended that fasting for 18-25 days could dissolve it.

His cure rate was ranked at about 90%, and many physicians couldn't believe it until they tried it for themselves. The only problem with the fasting practices was that there's a limit to how much a person can do it. Long-term results were required.

In 1916, Dr. McMurray told the New York Medical Journal he'd treated epileptic patients successfully by prescribing a fasting and starch/sugar-free diet for them since 1912.

In 1921, Rollin Woodyatt, an endocrinologist found out fasting wasn't the only method of producing ketones in the body. He presented that the process could be gotten with a low-carb and high-fat diet.

Woodyatt found out the liver produced the water-soluble compounds (acetone, acetoacetate, and β-hydroxybutyrate) known as ketone bodies, if the body was starved or when a high-fat and low-carb diet was followed. Later that same year, Dr. Russell Morse Wilder coined the term "ketogenic diet" and used it to treat epileptic patients.

Shortly after the name of the diet was coined, it went dark for about 60 years, mostly because of the rise of newer antiepileptic drugs. Doctors focused more on the pills since it was much more easier convincing kids to take them than forfeiting certain types of foods.

Revival and Publicity

The popularity of the ketogenic diet has been mostly due to the publicity created by certain famous individuals. In the mid-90s, Jim Abrahams (a Hollywood producer) had a son whose epilepsy was controlled effectively by the ketogenic diet. He then went on to create the Charlie Foundation to promote the therapeutic regimen and spread the word.

The appearances on NBC's program, *Dateline*, and the Meryl Streep movie, *First Do No Harm*, helped the diet to gain more traction. The the Charlie Foundation also sponsored a multicenter research study (its results were announced in 1996) that marked the beginning of new scientific interest in the diet.

Along the same line, various possible therapeutic uses of the diet were studied for several other neurological disorders like Alzheimer's, Autism, and Parkinson's, among others.

Over the years, various adaptations have been made to the ketogenic diet to support different lifestyle choices. One of the popular adjustments to the diet is the keto-vegan choice that allows non-meat/dairy product users to benefit from the diet.

Chapter Two

What is the Keto Vegan Diet?

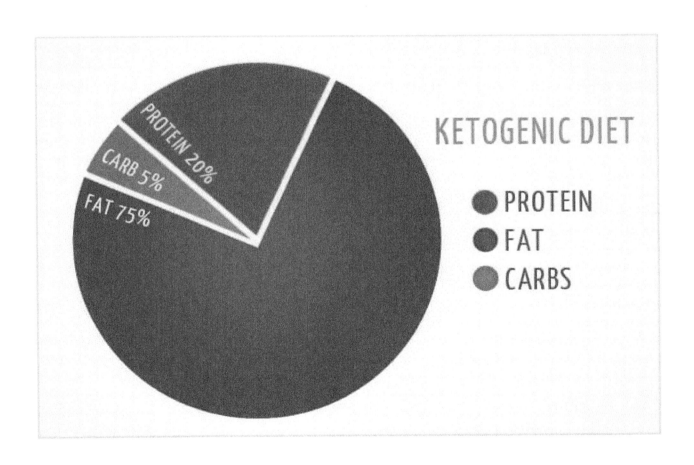

Before we describe what the Keto Vegan diet means, the terms "Vegan" and "Keto" need to be clarified. Just like vegetarians, vegans don't consume any animal product (meat, fish, birds, sea foods, etc.). But unlike them, they also steer clear from eggs, dairy, and any food that contains any trace of animal products as part of its ingredients.

A lot of vegans tend to avoid gelatin (derived from bones), fish oil supplements, casein (milk protein), or refined sugar since some brands use whitening agents like cow bones.

Like we explained earlier, ketogenic diets started as a treatment for epilepsy in the 1920s, even though the benefits have long since spread to other aspects of the body. The process of restricting carbohydrate intake and relying mostly on dietary fats tends to cause the liver to convert the fat into molecules (ketones), which are used as fuel for the body.

The best way to know when the body is undergoing ketosis is when the ketones rise above a particular threshold in the urine or during a breath test.

The simplest way to define this merge of diets is one that's free of meat, fish, or chicken that restricts carbohydrates. One of the perks of this dietary regime is that the individual gets all the benefits from the diet while lessening their carbon footprint, improving general health, and avoiding animal abuse.

Carbohydrates, in the keto vegan diet, are generally reduced to less than 50g each day to attain and maintain ketosis. It is a metabolic process in which the body burns up fat for fuel instead of using the stored glucose. Following this keto-vegan diet has been shown to reduce the risk of various heart conditions, including diabetes and several kinds of heart conditions.

One of the main reason individuals undergo ketosis is for sustained energy, which occurs when little amounts of carbs are consumed. Consuming a minimal amount of carbohydrates allows the insulin levels to remain steady, unlike when following a carb-based diet.

A stable blood sugar prevents you from going through afternoon crashes that make you feel like falling asleep at your work desk. Studies show that keto vegan diets effectively controls the blood sugar more than the standard low-calorie diet that boasts high-carb levels.

The keto vegan diet is one that has you eating from a low-carb and high-fat menu that's devoid of any animal product. While in theory, the process might sound simple enough for some people, the keto and vegan approach could be contradictory in reality.

The standard practice for keto dieters is consuming low amounts of carbs, and high quantities of meat, fish, and poultry. But this tactic wouldn't work for vegans since they avoid all that. The go-to foods for vegans are meat substitutes and high-protein legumes, but the carb content makes it unsuitable for making the keto diet successful.

The key here is balancing the two options. The goal of the keto vegan dieter should be to eat lots of plant-based fats, some plant-based proteinic foods, and a minimal amount of carbohydrates.

Health Concerns

While there are people who become vegans and avoid eating meat because of their concern for the animals slaughtered and the environment, there are also the ones who choose the lifestyle because they feel it's a healthier option.

Most of the time, vegan diets consist of high levels of starch, legumes, and grains, which aren't particularly suitable for individuals with diabetes who wish to control their blood sugar without the help of medication. Some people even tend to feel hungry when they stick to the low-fat and high-carb vegan eating practices. The keto-vegan diet is an excellent idea for persons who wish to avoid meat and yet derive the benefits of ketogenic living.

On a side note, there's a possibility of becoming deficient in some nutrients like protein and a few essential fats, minerals, and vitamins while following the vegan keto diet. It all depends on the type of foods you consume and diet you're following. The more it's restricted, the more your chances of developing one or more deficiencies increases.

The ketogenic diet can be incorporated into most of the vegan lifestyles. Although, the more liberal your choices, the more enjoyable your mealtimes could become. While it's easy to start a keto-vegan diet, it's vital that you're aware of the risks and restrictions before boarding the train.

Why Choose the Keto Vegan Diet

Before setting out to select a dietary style, exercise regime, or any other health choice, it's essential that we know what we want in the first place.

Whatever plan you pick needs to reflect what you're looking for in life. It should be able to give you what you want. Most people have different reasons for embarking on the keto diet. For some individuals, they need it to increase their energy levels and increase mental clarity and improvement of cognition skills. Several others want to improve the way they look (increase muscles or reduce body fat).

How the Diet Works

How to Follow a Vegan Keto Diet: Pros and Cons

Pro: Carb Restriction
A danger in keeping a vegan diet is a heavy reliance on carbohydrates; adding keto to veganism reduces carb intake drastically, serving as a natural check to excessive carb consumption.

Con: Fewer Protein Sources
Vegan dieters on their own sometimes struggle to get enough protein from plant-based sources, but with a calorie cap on that as well, it will be difficult to find the amount of protein needed without exceeding the calorie limit.

Pro: Weight Loss
The keto diet burns fat and cuts down on inflammation in the digestive system caused by gluten and sugar intake. Veganism, too, lowers the risk of obesity.

Con: Limited Food Choice
The amount of high-fat plant-based foods is low, so when looking for plant-based foods with enough fat and protein that are also low in carbs, it's a very short list.

Pro: Health Benefits
Vegan diets show a 75% lower risk of high blood pressure and a 78% reduction of risk for type 2 diabetes. The ketogenic diet in a study on obese children caused more weight/fat loss and lowered their risk of obesity-related diseases.

When an individual begins the keto diet process, they put their body into a fat-burning state of ketosis which requires that they get 80-90% of their daily calories from fat, 5-10% from carbohydrates, and 5-15% from proteins. Since a lot of people get at least half of their daily caloric contents from carbs, this diet provides a major shift from what they're used to along the way.

Transitioning to a keto-vegan based diet could be tricky for some vegans especially if they'd developed the habit of loading up on pasta and other heavy carb items. But in the end, the process would be beneficial for them to cut back on the processed foods they'd gotten so used to consuming.

The best way to navigate the dietary process successfully lies solely on figuring out which kinds of foods fit within the ketogenic and vegan limitations.

Observing the Keto-Vegan Diet in a Healthy Way

Since there's no getting around the fact you'll be deficient in some major nutrients because of the kinds of food you'll be eating, it's recommended that you load up on their equivalents. What this simply means is to get your daily dose of vitamin B12, you need to incorporate cheese into your meal plan, eggs or its substitutes for vitamin D, and leafy veggies like kale for calcium.

You might also want to consider easing up on your vegan strictness a little bit and eating fish (ones caught in the wild) if you don't do that already, mainly because they're a great source of protein and Omega 3s.

The keto-vegan diet won't necessarily be easy to follow since it combines two already restrictive diets. Very few people would be able to stick with it until the end of their program, but the ones who do end up benefiting immensely

from it. One of the few ways to make it work is to start small. It means gradually reducing your carbohydrate intake one day at a time instead of going full-blown keto-vegan overnight. This process will prevent an immediate shock to your system, which is pivotal in a successful diet.

Lots of vegans rely mostly on grains and legumes to meet up with their daily dose of required micronutrients in every meal. When the food they'd become reliant on becomes restricted, as well as seafood and meat, it's up to them to ensure that they consume foods with the right amounts of iron, omega-3 fatty acids, calcium, potassium, vitamin D and B12.

Rules to Follow in the Keto Vegan Diet

- The total consumption of carbs should be limited to no more than 35g per day (at least 5%).
- Meat, fish, poultry, eggs, dairy, or any other form of animal products should be eliminated totally from your meal.
- Consume more low-carb vegetables.
- At least 75% of your daily calories should be gotten from plant-based fats.
- About 20% of calories should be acquired from plant-based proteins.
- Start taking supplements for food nutrients you're not getting enough of (iron, zinc, taurine, Vitamin B6, B12 and D3, DHA, and EPA).

Chapter Three

Scientific Studies

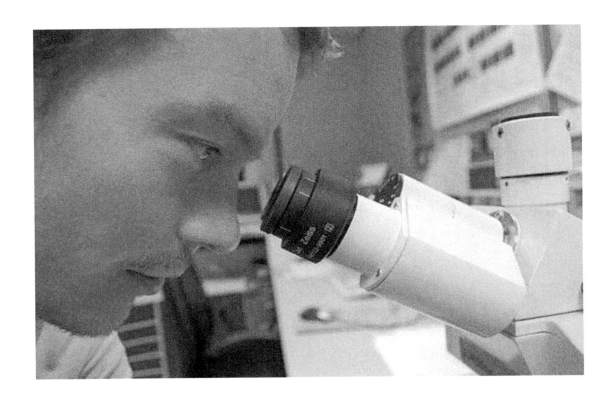

In the human body, carbs are stored as glycogen, which makes it the preferred energy source. Due to the excessive consumption of starchy foods, there's a steady supply to the energy reserves. And as soon as the carbs are eliminated from the diet, the body quickly uses up the stored supply.

If after a few days the carbohydrate reserve isn't replenished, the body enters into a metabolic state known as ketosis. This situation basically means your body is using up the stored fat for energy since there's no glycogen or carbohydrates.

When the glycogen stores are used up, the body tends to look for alternative sources – fat. This process is known as beta-oxidation, where the fatty acid molecules are broken down, and acetyl-CoA (used in carbohydrate, protein, and lipid metabolism for producing energy) increases.

When there's an upsurge of acetyl-CoA, the body goes through the citric acid cycle (the Krebs cycle) in the mitochondria. It combines with Oxaloacetic acid to form citric acid or citrate, which is essential for metabolism. Citrate goes on to cause the spontaneous breakdown of acetoacetate (a ketone body) which the liver stores, and then it'll be used as an energy source for the body.

The large amount of fatty foods consumed during the keto vegan diet helps in minimizing hunger cravings. It allows the individual to feel full for more extended periods during the day to reduce the amount of food they eat during the process.

Research shows vegans have the tendency to be thinner than their non-vegan counterparts, and also have lower body mass indexes (BMI). And their cholesterol levels also tend to be lower.

Most of the studies carried out on the vegan ketogenic diet show that it led to significant weight loss when followed strictly. The process is often restrictive and this makes it difficult for some people to sustain them for long periods.

Studies show for every 100 persons who adopt the diet, around 98 of them will fail because not everyone has what it takes to continue on the journey.

Reaching ketosis can be difficult for most individuals. While following the vegan keto diet, about 70-90% of the recommended calories are gotten from fat. The number of carbohydrates permitted daily is about 10-35g, even though many people still try to push it to 40 or 50 grams.

The Science Behind Low Carb High Fat Diets (LCHF)

Several kinds of studies are involved when considering diets and nutrition. Some of them include;

- Observational
- Large analysis
- Epidemiology (study and analysis of distribution and determinants)
- Randomized control trials (RCTs)

A study carried out showed that HDL increased drastically in people who had started the keto vegan diet, while the LDL reduced significantly.

The Hunger Hormone

Ghrelin also called the hunger hormone is a particular substance that's secreted in the body. To stimulate an individual's appetite, ghrelin increases

substantially. Several theories propose that ketosis decreases the appetite by suppressing the increase of the hormone.

Diabetes

Several researches conducted reveals that people suffering from diabetes benefit uniquely from this low-car and high-fat diet in various ways. The nature of the disease involves the inability of the patient to process carbs sufficiently based on the inadequacy of the insulin function.

Decreasing the amount of carbs consumed daily tends to be beneficial for the disease. Ketosis has also been shown to improve insulin functions, which end up becoming useful for the persons.

The vegan keto diet is far superior to other low-calorie diets in terms of improving glycemic controls and loss of weight in individuals living with diabetes.

Neurology

A professor in the neurological field (Swanson) tried inducing a ketogenic state in mice suffering from stoke and was stunned by the results. He discovered that blocking the glucose metabolism worked in suppressing specific inflammatory genes, which then helped the stroke to heal.

He deduced that the anti-inflammatory effect of the ketosis that was discovered in the stroke recovery was most likely the same one that helped kids with certain types of seizures.

Cutting back on carbs has multiple metabolic benefits. And since the body processes the carbs remaining more efficiently, it ends up requiring less insulin.

Most of the scientific studies carried out on ketosis have been done mostly on mice and small animals since it is relatively difficult maintaining the state and avoiding carbs. Very few clinical studies have used human subjects apart from the ones done for preventing seizures in epileptic patients.

Chapter Four

Physical/Psychological Benefits and Contraindications

PRO'S OF A VEGAN KETO DIET

WHOLEFOODS

Processed foods are loaded with refined carbohydrates hence on this diet you will be eating a whole food diet which means more nutritious ingredients, such as avocados, green vegetables, olives and hemp.

SUGAR

Obviously on a carb restricted diet, any forms of added sugar are avoided, which is great since we know sugar is not a healthy ingredient and a major cause of lifestyle related disease! Sugar is also very addictive, hence cutting it out strictly can help curb the cravings.

HOME COOKED

Since eating out is difficult to do and still achieve your macro goals, you will most likely be cooking most of your food at home which means you can control what goes into your food.

LOW PROTEIN

A true keto diet is actually moderate to low in protein. This is good since high protein diets can damage the kidneys, plus a diet high in animal based protein is accelerates aging mechanisms/decreases longevity.

LESS HUNGER

A common side effect of the keto-diet is decreased feelings of hunger and increased satiety (feeling satisfied). This is positive for people who tend to act too frequently on hunger cues.

HIGH FIBRE

Contrary to a standard keto diet, a plant based diet is still high in fibre. High fat foods like avocado, hemp, chia, flax, & nuts contain great amounts of fibre, + the leafy greens!

The goal of the keto vegan diet is for the individual to acquire more calories from fats and proteins than from carbs; this works by depleting the body's store of sugar so it'll begin breaking down the fats and proteins for energy.

If you're on a heavy-carb diet, your body tends to continually go through the cycle of converting the carbohydrates into glucose, which ends up increasing the blood sugar levels. There's an initial surge of energy which later gets depleted; resulting in more cravings.

Unlike the carb diet, being in ketosis is like burning logs of wood instead of adding kindling to the fire. The logs (fats) last longer and burn steadily while the kindling (carbs) burn bright for a little while before disappearing.

Individuals on the high-fat diet have consistent energy levels minus the energy spikes, and they don't experience the same kinds if cravings they used to have with a high-carb diet.

Other than the increase in energy levels and reduction in hunger cravings, there are several other benefits of sticking with this particular diet, and some of them include;

Enhancing the Overall Health of the Heart

One of the main causes of death in the country results from heart diseases. Various health conditions can trigger it, although an unhealthy diet, lack of exercise, and obesity tend to be the major causes.

Research shows that when this form of diet is followed in the right manner, it tends to improve the health of the heart by reducing cholesterol significantly. You might want to consider replacing pork rinds with avocados as a healthy fat.

A study conducted revealed that High-Density Lipoprotein (HDL) – which is the good form of cholesterol, increased significantly within individuals who adopted the vegan keto diet, while their Low-Density Lipoprotein (LDL) decreased drastically.

Lots of people might believe having a high-fat diet isn't necessarily good for the heart, but that's not the case here. Not only is consuming healthy fats safe for the body, but it also has long-term benefits too.

Continuously sticking with a keto vegan diet reduces the amount of fat molecules and triglycerides linked to heart diseases from circulating inside the bloodstream.

In most cases, heart diseases arise when excess carbs are consumed, which then lead to an increase in triglyceride levels. The keto vegan diet helps in limiting the number of carbohydrates consumed daily.

It Helps with Weight Loss

More work is required to turn fat into energy than with carbohydrates. As a result of this, keto-vegan diets tend to speed up the process of losing weight; that's why it's best for individuals who intend to shed a few pounds. Since the keto-vegan diet is rich in protein, it doesn't leave the dieter hungry as other ones do.

When the calorie intake is reduced during the keto-vegan diet, the body starts burning its fat stores to make ketones. One of the features that make it highly effective for weight loss is its natural appetite-suppressing effect.

Lots of individuals adopt the keto vegan diet as an effective means of managing their weight. The low-carb regime allows the body to go into a perpetual state of ketosis; forcing it to burn fat until a healthy body weight is attained.

While undergoing this diet, the need for intensive exercises is reduced since the diet is already making the body burn fat instead of the carbs consumed. The stomach fat – which is usually the hardest one to burn during regular dietary restrictions, disappears faster in ketosis.

Lowers Blood Sugar

Consuming foods with high carbohydrate contents tend to cause blood sugar or glucose levels to increase at a rapid pace. As a result, the pancreas produces lots of insulin which is used to transport the glucose to the cells for either storage purposes or to burn for fuel.

Eating large quantities of carbs or processed foods daily, causes glucose and insulin levels to continue spiking, which ends up causing more problems for the body.

Since the diet is quite low in carbs, it helps in reducing the blood sugar considerably. It's also great for reversing diabetes and improving insulin sensitivity.

The low-carb diet ensures a sugar-free dietary plan which decreases the risk of developing diabetes for people with the genetic marker. Individuals who already suffer from the disease can use the diet to lower their insulin dosages or eliminate medications completely.

While on the vegan keto diet, you consume fatty foods that don't affect the blood sugar or cause the insulin levels to rise.

Provides Anti-Inflammatory Protection

A lot of chronic diseases that plague individuals are as a result of one form of inflammation or the other (diabetes, arthritis, cancer, cardiovascular diseases, etc.). Studies carried out revealed the keto diet provides the body with antioxidant and anti-inflammatory protection, which is excellent at preventing most of these diseases.

Making the switch to keto vegan means you've agreed to turn your back on processed foods that cause inflammation (like pasta, bread, cereals) and damage the gut. You replace those foods with nourishing fats, clean protein sources, and fresh vegetables that heal inflammations.

Research shows that there's a link between inflammation and depression; which means that consuming anti-inflammatory foodstuffs will have a direct effect on the mood. The study showed depressed individuals possess higher levels of pro-inflammatory cytokines (the body releases them in response to inflammation).

Neuroprotective Functions

The brain is made up of about 60% fatty tissues, and it needs tons of healthy fats to keep it running. Various studies have revealed that omega-3 fatty acids can reduce depression by a significant amount. In one of the studies, EPA and DHA (types of omega-3 acids) were shown to aid in secreting serotonin – the neurotransmitter that regulates people's moods. Low levels of serotonin have been linked to depression.

Although this area is still undergoing more research to determine the full range of benefits, some research suggests keto diets offer various protections for the brain. They may help in the treatment of some sleep disorders or the creation of preventive measures for diseases like Parkinson's or Alzheimer's.

The keto vegan diet helps in clearing beta-amyloid protein, which tends to stick together and prevent the fast and effectual flow of brain signals.

One particular study revealed that kids following the keto-vegan diet developed improved cognitive functions and alertness; it improves critical thinking skills. High carb diets often lead to spikes in blood sugar, which tends to lead to brain fog. The antioxidant and anti-inflammatory action of ketones helps in protecting the brain against damage from free radicals.

Following a balanced diet that's rich in healthy fats, moderate in proteins, and low in carbohydrates protects the body's neurovascular functions and helps maintain excellent cognitive skills. Some evidence also shows the keto diet might even protect the brain during traumatic injuries and stroke.

Aids in Reducing Acne

There are multiple causes of acne, and one of them might be related to diet and blood sugar. Individuals who eat more processed and refined carbs might end up altering the gut bacteria, which tends to cause dramatic fluctuations in their blood sugar, which eventually affects skin health. The carbs cause inflammation in the body, which is one of the major reasons for the formation of acne.

The solution to some acne problems might be as simple as decreasing the daily intake of carbohydrates in the body. A high-glycemic diet often tends to worsen acne and cause breakouts to occur. Unlike carbs and sugar, which trigger pimples and other skin blemishes, good fats prevent the individual from having inflammatory acne and soothe dry skin.

It Reduces Seizures

The combination of protein, fats, and carbs tends to alter the way the body uses energy, which often results in ketosis (the elevated level of ketone in the bloodstream). There have been cases involving people with epilepsy where ketosis reduces the frequency of seizures in them.

While there are still some issues surrounding its efficacy, the keto-vegan diet tends to be more active on kids with focal seizures.

It Improves the Health of Women with Polycystic Ovarian Syndrome (PCOS)

PCOS is an endocrine disorder that results in enlarged ovaries with cysts. Studies show that a diet that's filled with high carbs can negatively affect individuals suffering from this condition.

Although more research is needed in this area, some clinical studies revealed the keto-vegan diet aided with hormone balance improved fasting insulin, and increased weight loss, among other things.

One of the best ways of achieving the benefits of the keto-vegan diet is by lowering your carb levels to below 50g each day while increasing your fat intake so that it comprises 65-80% of your diet. The macros can, however, be adjusted to fit every individual's specific needs and goals.

Lowering the Possibility of Metabolic Syndrome

The metabolic syndrome has been defined by the NHLB Institute as a group of risk factors that increase the risk for heart diseases and other health issues (stroke and diabetes).

Having three out of the five risk factors listed below means you'll be diagnosed with the syndrome;

- High blood sugar
- Increased blood pressure
- Low HDL cholesterol (the good fat)
- High triglyceride levels
- Abdominal obesity

About one-quarter of the American population have the syndrome.

A high-fat low-carb diet affects the way the body processes fats and reduces abdominal fat and triglycerides when it's compared to consuming low-fat foods. The vegan keto diet helps in reducing the risks of developing the metabolic syndrome and the various health defects associated with it.

Improving Endurance Performance

The oxidation of fat can be described as the process of breaking down fats (lipids) into smaller sizes so they can be converted into energy. The keto diet has been revealed to help highly-trained ultra-endurance athletes to increase the amount of fats their body breaks down and burns.

Studies conducted showed minimizing the intake of high-carbs improves health but doesn't limit the body's overall performance. A high-fat diet allows you to function or exercise for more extended periods while consuming very few calories.

Reducing Cancer Risk

Since a vegan diet is free from any form of meat, it improves the individual's chances of not getting cancer. Even in the face of all our technological advancements, there's still no cure for cancer. The best way to battle the disease is by maintaining a healthy lifestyle and proper metabolic functions.

Recent studies have revealed sugar feeds cancer cells. The keto vegan diet is designed to eliminate sugar from the system since the ketone bodies are used instead of glucose.

When carbs and glucose levels are reduced in the body, your system tends to starve the cancer cells that need them to grow. A low-carb diet has been known to slow down the growth of some kinds of brain tumors and also reduce the reappearance of certain types of breast cancer.

The vegan keto diet serves as both protection and prevention against cancer growth by reducing the consumption of carbs; replacing them with healthy fats.

Sleep Improvement

Another great feature of the keto vegan diet is that it improves sleep patterns. It allows individuals to stay alert all day and then enjoy a pleasant rest at night.

The sleep patterns end up changing due to the increase of good fats and the reduction of carbohydrates. Some researchers proposed the diet could affect the production of a chemical in the brain known as adenosine – which helps in regulating sleep.

Hormone-Stabilization

The hormones in the body serve as chemical messengers, and when there's an imbalance in the system, everything becomes chaotic. Unlike some other diets, the ketosis affects them in a good way.

Consumption of low-carbs and high-fats tend to lower the levels of insulin through the process of eliminating sugar in the diet. Other than that, leptin (the hormone that suppresses hunger) levels are reduced, which helps in regulating eating habits.

The keto vegan diet is especially great for women as it aids the pituitary glands in working better, regulating progesterone and thyroid, which helps in preventing progesterone deficiency and infertility.

Great for Eyesight and Improved Vision

The vegan ketogenic diet is rich in good fats and low in carbohydrates, which helps the retinal cells become healthier; preventing its degeneration. It's great for preventing progressive diseases that result in poor vision or blindness, glaucoma, and even cataracts.

Individuals on this diet increase their chances of reducing visual defects or even slowing down the progression of their present condition.

Apart from weight loss, the keto vegan diet has tons of other health benefits; you just have to try to determine what works for you.

Complications and Adverse Effects of the Diet

Almost everything good has a downside, and the keto-vegan diet isn't exempted from this rule. While it has excellent benefits, it's vital to note that remaining too long on the keto diet can have side effects on your health.

Individuals who follow the vegan keto diet long-term tend to increase the risk of developing the following conditions;

- The formation of kidney stones
- Severe weight-loss or the degeneration of muscle functions
- High level of acid within the blood (acidosis)
- Low blood sugar
- Constipation
- Sluggishness

Some of the minor symptoms might occur at the beginning of the diet as the body struggles to adjust to the new regime. Since the primary and preferred source of energy of the body and brain comes mostly from glucose, the sudden elimination of carbs might not sit well with the major organs.

Some reports have noted the diet results in a drop in libido during the early stages. During that period, the dieter would be experiencing carb withdrawal symptoms and, in some cases, the keto flu. It's essential to note the reduced libido symptom doesn't always happen to everyone; it's hard to come by.

Luckily, this feature doesn't last long because once the symptoms pass and the body adapts to the low-carb diet, the libido will reset itself and most likely become better than before. This loss of weight from the dietary restriction ends up improving the lifestyle of the individual.

Most individuals already know about the keto flu since it happens when the body tries to adapt to the change in diet. Symptoms of the flu could range from anything to headache, irritability, constipation, weakness, nausea, and vomiting.

Since there's no predicting how your body will react to a new diet like the keto-vegan one, it's always essential that you talk to a doctor or a nutritionist before proceeding with the plan. And if you can't handle the long-term dietary regimes, try sticking with the shorter plans. Make sure to remember that not everyone can participate in the vegan keto diet, especially if they have special health requirements.

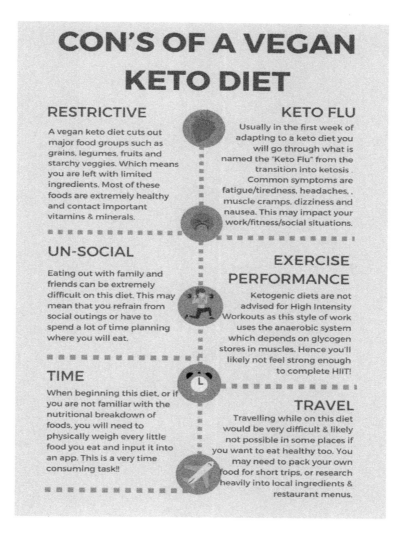

Chapter Five

Various Foods and Fruits (And Benefits)

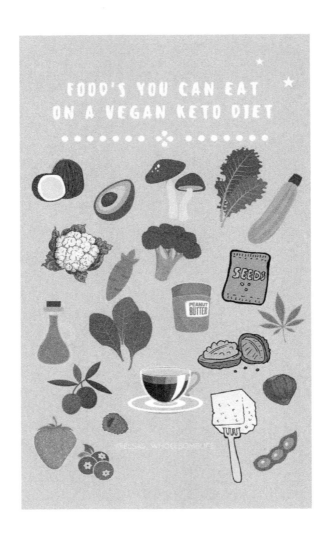

Unlike the individuals who embark on the ketogenic diet who have more food options, vegans trying out this regime have a slightly less amount in comparison. Since they can't rely on meat and poultry products for their supply of proteins, different plant alternatives are considered.

Most of the items listed in this section can easily be found in your typical grocery store. The acceptable choices of foods for keto-vegans with sufficient micronutrients include;

Nuts and Seeds

Pumpkin seeds	Chia seeds	Almonds	Sunflower seeds
Brazil nuts	Flax seeds	Peanuts	Dark chocolate (100%)
Hemp seeds	Walnuts	Pine nuts	Hazelnuts/filberts
Unsweetened cocoa			

(Almonds, Peanuts, and Pine nuts have high-carb content and should be eaten sparingly).

Walnuts:

1) They're rich in antioxidants which help in fighting oxidative damage to the body
2) Serve as a great source of omega-3s or alpha-linolenic acid (they have a higher content than any other nut)
3) They reduce inflammation of the cells

4) They help control appetite and hunger which makes it great for weight-control

5) Decrease cholesterol levels

Pumpkin seeds:

1) They help improve the symptoms associated with benign prostatic hyperplasia (BPH)

2) The seeds are rich in magnesium which is essential for healthy blood pressure levels

3) Tend to lower blood sugar levels

4) They contain high fiber content which is great for digestion

Dark chocolate:

1) The kinf with high cocoa content are often loaded with minerals and are quite nutritious

2) They contain a wide variety of powerful antioxidants (more than most foods)

3) They help in reducing blood pressure and flow

4) It increases HDL, protects LDL from oxidation, and reduces insulin resistance; improving its sensitivity

Chia seeds:

1) They contain very few calories while packing massive amounts of nutrients

2) They have rich-fiber contents

3) They serve as great sources of quality protein

4) Chia seeds are rich in magnesium, phosphorus, and calcium – all of which are essential for bone health

Vegetables

Broccoli	Shallots	Dandelion greens
Beets	Lettuce	Rhubarb
Kale	Zucchini	Mustard greens
Spinach	Turnips	Brussels sprouts
Celery	Eggplant	Squash (summer and winter)
Okra	Radishes	Swiss chard
Garlic	Cucumbers	Asparagus
Carrots	Mushrooms	Bell peppers
Onion		

(Brussels sprouts, kale, and squash-winter have high-carb content and should be eaten sparingly)

Broccoli:

1) Serves as a rich source of fiber, vitamins, and minerals
2) Contains numerous bioactive compounds that help in reducing body and tissue inflammation

3) They're useful for controlling blood sugar levels

4) Broccolis are great at lowering various cardiovascular diseases

5) They reduce constipation as they promote healthy digestion

Beets:

1) They're a great source of nitrates which is pretty good for the heart and blood pressure

2) They improve the flow of blood in the body which helps in moving oxygen around efficiently

3) Beets interfere with inflammatory signaling processes

4) They improve cognitive functions

5) They're great for vision and improve the immune system

Zucchini:

1) They're rich in antioxidants

2) Zucchini promotes healthy digestion and reduces constipation

3) They're great for weight loss regimes

4) The peel extracts help in keeping thyroid hormone levels stable

Mushrooms:

1) They boost vitamin D production

2) Since mushrooms are rich in selenium, they help reduce the risk of developing bladder cancer

3) They enhance functions of the immune system by protecting and healing body tissues

4) Mushrooms' serve as a great source of iron which is excellent at combating anemia symptoms

Fruits

Olives	Strawberries	Watermelon
Avocadoes	Raspberries	Tomatoes
Blueberries	Coconuts	Lemons
Limes	Cranberries	

(Blueberries have high-carb content and should be eaten sparingly)

Strawberries:

1) They boost the body's immune system
2) They act as detoxifiers which help in reducing gout and arthritis pain
3) Strawberries are great for boosting the production of leptin and adiponectin (fat-burning hormones) and promoting weight loss.
4) They help in reducing congenital disabilities during pregnancy

Avocadoes:

1) It contains all the necessary nutrients and more
2) Avocadoes produce more potassium than bananas and help in maintaining the electrical gradients of the cells
3) It's a high-fat food that monounsaturated fatty acids
4) They tend to lower triglyceride and cholesterol levels

Tomatoes:

1) They're low-carb fruits
2) They serve as great sources of vitamins and minerals
3) Tomatoes have protective effects on the inner layer of the blood vessels and aid in reducing risks of clotting
4) They're highly beneficial for healthy skins

Olives:

1) They're rich antioxidant sources
2) Reduce blood pressure
3) Improve bone health and quality
4) Good sources of essential vitamins and minerals

Nut and Seed Butters

Peanut butter	Hazelnut butter	Coconut butter
Almond butter	Pecan butter	Sunflower seed butter
Macadamia nut butter		

Coconut butter:

1) It's easily absorbed and transported directly to the liver for metabolism
2) It's great for weight loss

3) Coconut butter has antibacterial, antiviral, and antifungal properties

4) It has fewer calories than most vegetable oils and also increases the HDL levels in the body

Almond butter:

1) It's a great source of healthy monounsaturated fats which help in lowering the risk of heart diseases

2) It keeps the blood sugar levels stable

3) Reduces the risk of developing gallstones in women

4) They have antioxidant properties

Macadamia nut butter:

1) Reduces blood pressure

2) Helps in controlling blood sugar levels

3) Increases HDL cholesterol

4) They're useful in improving bowel movement regularity

Peanut butter:

1) It's rich in essential nutrients and fats

2) It's great for bodybuilding

3) It helps in managing blood sugar levels

Healthy Oils

Avocado oil   Coconut oil   Macadamia nut oil

| Almond oil | Cacao butter | MCT oil |
| Flaxseed oil | Hazelnut oil | Olive oil |

Medium-Chain Triglyceride (MCT) Oil:

1) It increases the release of the two hormones responsible for making the body feel full (leptin and peptide YY)
2) It's an instant source of energy for the body and brain cells
3) MCTs help in reducing the buildup of lactate levels; making it great for athletes
4) Beneficial for managing epileptic seizures, Alzheimer's and even autism

Flaxseed oil:

1) It contains a healthy amount of omega-3 fatty acids
2) Helps in reducing cancer cell growth
3) It's effective at treating diarrhea and constipation by acting as both an antidiarrheal agent, and a laxative
4) Improves hydration and smoothness of the skin

Olive Oil:

1) It possesses strong and effective anti-inflammatory properties
2) It plays a role in preventing strokes
3) Acts against bacteria

Cacao butter:

1) It's rich in fatty acids

2) It reduces the risk of developing any cardiovascular disease and improves the overall health of the heart
3) It lowers inflammatory biomarkers
4) Reduces the risk of getting diabetes and stroke when consumed weekly

Sauces and Condiments

Soy sauce/tamari	Chili sauce	Vinegar
Hot sauce	Hummus	Tomato sauce
Mustard	Salsa	

(Hummus has a high-carb content and should be eaten sparingly)

Fridge Staples for Keto Vegans

Dairy-free yogurt and cheese	Pickles	Micro-greens
Apple cider vinegar	Tofu	Seitan (wheat meat)
All kinds of sprouts	Tempeh	

(The dairy-free yogurt and cheese have higher carb content, while Tofu, Seitan, and Tempeh are rich sources of protein).

Tofu:

1) It's a good source of protein seeing as it contains all the essential amino acids
2) It helps in lowering LDLs
3) Its antioxidant properties tend to prevent cancer cell growth
4) Enhances kidney functions and increases bone mineral density

Tempeh:

1) It serves as a great source of protein and is rich in several other nutrients
2) It's rich in prebiotics (promotes the growth of essential bacteria in the gut)
3) Lowers cholesterol levels
4) It reduces oxidative stress

Pantry Staples

Coconut flour	Nutritional yeast	Baking soda and powder
Almond flour	Artichoke hearts	Coconut milk (canned, full fat)

Cocoa powder   Vanilla extract (no sugar)   Jackfruit (canned in brine and green)

Consume Very Low-Carb Vegetables at Least Twice Daily

Several keto-friendly greens provide a nice dose of fiber, taste great, and also allow you to meet your daily micronutrient needs. Some of them include;

- Spinach – serves as a rich source of iron, potassium, and magnesium
- Avocado – rich in fiber, potassium, and magnesium
- Zucchini – serves as a great source of vitamin B6, C, and potassium too
- Cauliflower – a perfect keto-friendly substitute for mashed potatoes and rice and contains high amounts of vitamin C and fiber
- Brussels sprouts – contain high levels of Folate, potassium, and vitamin C.

Using Healthy Oils for Cooking or Salad Dressings

Healthy fats not only have a delicious taste, but they also improve the texture of the food while ensuring that you feel satisfied and full for several hours in a day. They're also essential for the adequate absorption of the fat-soluble vitamins (A, D, E, and K).

It's crucial you select the healthiest types of fatty foods and oil since they contribute to most of your calories on the keto diet. Oils derived from vegetables and seeds like sunflower, corn, and canola oil tend to be highly processed and have often been linked to inflammation.

Your best bet is to choose healthy keto fats such as olive oil, butter, avocado and coconut oil for the preparation of your meals and dressings. Also, herbs and spices like basil, cinnamon, and rosemary serve as additional sources of micronutrients for your keto-vegan needs.

Consume a Variety of Fatty Foods

There's no escaping it since this class of food constitutes the majority part of the keto-vegan diet. And that's why it's crucial to select the ones with the highest-quality and healthiest. A variety of fats will ensure that your body gets everything it needs. You need to be careful when choosing the right one to incorporate into your diet plan since some are essential, and a few others aren't.

Essential Polyunsaturated Fatty Acids

The essential fatty acids are the ones that the body needs to attain from food items since they can't produce them. They're crucial for healthy skin and brain functions, the regulation of inflammation, and several other purposes.

Out of all the fatty acids, only two are essential

1. Alpha-linolenic acid (Omega-3 fatty acid)
2. Linoleic acid (Omega-6 fatty acid)

Since linoleic acid is more common, lots of people already get enough of them, unlike the Omega-3 fatty acids which are much harder to get. Walnuts, chia seeds, olive oil, and flaxseed remain some of the best vegetarian sources for Omega-3 fats. Note that the body needs large amounts of these essential fats to convert it into a useable form, so you'd need to consume reasonable amounts regularly.

Saturated Fats

Researchers have discovered that the roles of saturated fats have been exaggerated for too long. Almost every health disorder was blamed on them, from heart attacks, strokes, to atherosclerosis. Just like everything else, there are good and bad parts of it; even though most times we only hear about the bad ones.

Saturated fats serve as a valuable tool for increasing ketones during a keto-vegan diet. The medium-chain triglycerides (MCTs) which are a select type of fats, have been proven to raise ketones. They're sent directly to the liver to be used up for energy since they don't need digestive enzymes to digest them. MCT sources include – palm kernel oil (52%), coconut oil (68%), and MCT oil (100%). Dairy serves as another source of MCT, but since the concentration is too low, you won't notice any particular health impact.

Monounsaturated Fats

MUFAs are regarded as a healthy form of fat since multiple studies have revealed the protective effects on the heart and other metabolic functions. MUFA sources include; high-oleic sunflower oil (85%), olive oil (75%), canola oil (60%), and safflower oil (77%). Avocados, dark chocolate, most nuts, basil pesto, and pumpkin seeds serve as other great options. Incorporating these fatty acids into your keto-vegan diet goes a long way in affecting your health positively

Chapter Six

Foods to Avoid during the Keto Vegan Diet

It's already hard enough restricting the consumption of carbs on a standard ketogenic diet. Bringing the keto vegan diet into the mix adds a whole new level to the process.

Vegans can't use meat and dairy products for their protein requirements, so they need to be creative when using substitutes for these food items.

Here's a list of items to avoid during the vegan keto diet;

> **Grains** – corn, rice, cereals, wheat, pasta
> **Fruits** – oranges, bananas, apples
> **Legumes** – peas, lentils, black beans
> **Sugar** – maple syrup, honey, agave, refined sugar, corn syrup
> **Tubers** – yams, potatoes
> **High-carb nuts –** cashews, pistachios, chestnuts
> Meat, fish, eggs, poultry, dairy, and other animal products
> Trans fats and refined vegetable oils (they promote inflammation in the body)

Keto Vegan Dairy Replacements

Most times, when you search for recipes for the keto diet, you'll see lots of ones that feature eggs and various dairy products. Thankfully, there are keto vegan-friendly replacements for egg and dairy products.

Dairy Foods	Substitutes
Milk	Almond and Coconut Milk

Cream	Coconut cream
Butter	Vegan butter/coconut oil
Eggs (for meals)	Silken tofu and vegetables
Eggs (for cooking)	Flaxseed (add water in a 1:3 ratio)

Grains/Starches	Substitutes
Rice	Cauliflower rice
Pasta	Zucchini and Shirataki noodles
Sandwich bread	Lettuce wraps
Tortillas	Flax tortillas
Mashed potatoes	Cauliflower mashed potatoes
Cereal	Chia pudding, flax granola
Waffles	Almond flour waffles
Oatmeal	Noatmeal (made from coconut flour, coconut butter, protein powder)
Pancakes	Peanut butter pancakes

Substitutes

Snacks

Chips	Dehydrated vegetables (kale chips)
Crackers	Chia seed crackers

Desserts	Substitutes
Ice cream	Low-carb sorbet, Avocado ice cream
Brownies	Avocado, almond flour, macadamia nut
Pudding	Avocado pudding

You can easily replace sour cream and yogurt with a nut-based yogurt. It's also possible to find cashew, almond, or coconut milk yogurt at local health food stores. But it's always best to check if they contain any hidden carbs or sugars; steer clear of the ones that do.

When trying to get dairy products that are keto vegan-friendly, ensure that you're not getting ones with unhealthy ingredients like hydrogenated oils, processed sugar, or hidden carbs. Thankfully, the rate of availability of high-quality vegan-friendly alternatives has increased over the last few years.

Flaxseed

The ones that have been ground smoothly tend to make excellent binders. The nutty flavor works quite well with recipes for pancakes or almond flour baked goods. One tablespoon of ground flaxseed and about three tablespoons of water replaces one egg successfully.

Baking Soda and Vinegar

They are great to use when making fluffier desserts. One tablespoon of white vinegar mixed with a teaspoon of baking soda serves as a substitute for one egg.

Silken Tofu

This version of tofu is silkier and softer, making it an excellent replacement for eggs. Even though it doesn't have the same kind of flavor real eggs have, it makes baked goods dense and can be used for bread, cakes, and brownies.

Although, if you don't care so much for these egg-substitutes, it's okay to skip right to the ready-made vegan options made by different companies. They're great and all, but most of them don't contain as much protein and fats as required for your daily content; which means you'd have to make up for them through other dietary means.

There are a few vegan burgers and other "meats" that can be found in most grocery stores in the country. And if you decide to go for any one of them, it's essential you carefully read the nutrition facts and ingredients before committing to them.

If it turns out that any of the products contain high-carbs, refined sugars, or any other potentially harmful ingredient, walk away from it. You could easily search for items with the lowest possible carb content, simple ingredients, and high-fat and protein contents.

Learning to Restrict Carbs from your Diet

One of the few ways to get into ketosis and ensure you remain there is to limit the net carb intake to at least 20g daily. What this means for your dietary needs is you'll need to stay away from lots of the popular vegan protein sources like quinoa, legumes, pulses, and buckwheat.

Since most of these foodstuffs have high carbohydrate contents, they need to be excluded to maintain the keto-vegan lifestyle. You might also want to avoid dairy products, milk, starchy veggies, and fruits; except maybe for some berries.

Cutting out bread, rice, grains, and pasta from your diet will reduce your carb intake by a substantial amount. Some of the fruits on the list might have to be eaten sparingly too since some of them contain carbohydrates.

It's possible to trick your brain into believing it's consuming some of your favorite carbs if you feel like your resolve to remain on the keto vegan diet is wavering. Zucchini could be sliced into strings to sort of look like pasta. Or grate the cauliflower into rice forms or even boil and mash like potatoes. The trick is to spice up the meals to make them enticing and fun to prepare and eat.

Chapter Seven

Importance of Calories

Everyone needs calories in their diet. They're crucial to human health. The key here is consuming it at the right amount. In the biological point of view, calories are considered as units of energy, while in nutrition, they're the energy people get from the foods and drinks they consume. They're also considered as the energy used up during physical activities.

Depending on our age, sex, size, or activity levels, we all require different amounts of energy every day. Most people get more than 11% of their daily calories from unhealthy fast foods. These kinds are often high in energy but have little or no nutritional values and provide empty calories.

Calories aren't always particular to foods and drinks. Anything that has energy contained within it has calories too. There are two types of calories; a small one (cal) and the large one (kcal). 1kcal is equal to a thousand calories.

The calorie content that's usually found at the back of food items refers to kilocalories; which means a small 250 kcal chocolate bar contains 250,000 calories.

The average daily calorie requirement for a man is about 2700 kcal, while that of a woman is 2200 kcal. Since people have different basal metabolic rates, not everyone has the same requirement. It

might be small for some others and significant for the remaining ones.

The body requires a healthy amount of calories to survive because, without them, the primary organs would fail and die. If everyone consumed the needed amounts daily, there wouldn't be problems, and we'd all live healthy lives. But that isn't always the case.

Consuming more calories than the body needs tends to lead to weight gain. They are essential in that they determine whether you lose weight, gain more, or maintain the one you already have. The total calories consumed and their source plays a significant role in how they impact your health.

Energy

The process where the body converts calories gotten from food into usable energy is known as metabolism. Regardless of what we're doing, our bodies always need energy; even while sleeping. They're used for breathing, repairing damaged cells, circulating blood for transport purposes in the body, and taking care of other bodily functions.

Ensuring that you eat the right amount and kind of food is a great way to make sure the body gets enough energy for working and development purposes. You can easily calculate how much calories your body needs by using a food plan to map out what you eat and what it contains.

Weight Control

The best way to ensure a stable weight is by keeping the number of consumed calories balanced with the one you burn daily through metabolism and other physical activities. Extra weight is gained when you take in more calories than the body can handle at a particular time; it then stores the spare ones as fat.

- One gram of fat tends to contain 9 kcal

- One gram of protein contains 4 kcal
- One gram of carbohydrate contains 4 kcal

Empty Calories

These can be considered as the calories that provide energy but add very little or no nutritional value at all to the body. Foods that provide empty calories don't contain amino acids, vitamins, dietary fiber, minerals, or even antioxidants. They tend to come from added sugars and solid fats.

While the solid fats and sugars make the foods and drinks they're added to more enjoyable and sweeter, they often increase the calorie count and contribute to weight gain.

Some of the primary sources of empty calories include;

- Pastries
- Cakes
- Cookies
- Donuts
- Ice cream
- Ribs
- Sausages
- Cheese
- Pizza
- Bacon
- Hot dogs
- Energy drinks

- Soda
- Fruit drinks

Caloric Balance

This factor plays a vital role in determining an individual's overall health. You can consider yourself to be within the balance when, over a specified period, if the number of calories consumed matches the amount you burn through your body's metabolism and physical activities.

When you're going through caloric excess, you tend to consume more calories than your body can handle at the time, which leads to accumulation and weight gain.

In contrast to that, calorie deficit means your body is burning up more than it's taking in, which leads to loss of body mass. Most times, caloric excess is required for growing children since they're using the energy derived in developing their minds and bodies. Still, there's always a need to moderate things.

A healthy and properly balanced diet that's designed to support all the body's physiological processes should offer 45–65% of calories from carbohydrates, 20-35% from fats, and the remaining 10-35% from protein. But during the keto vegan diet, you might have to switch up things a little bit since you need fewer carbs and more fats.

Counting calories has its pros as well as cons. It's essential to be aware of how much we consume, but it should also be done with moderation; without taking things too far. For one, being aware of your consumed calories tends to increase your nutritional awareness, and takes you a step further in making better food choices. Also, knowing how much calories are used up during exercises can be a useful motivator for some people.

It's also useful to note that various foods require different amounts of energy to digest and utilize them in the body. This phenomenon is referred to as the Thermic Effect of Food (TEF). Simply put, TEF means that out of all the food we eat, some of the calories contained there are often used during the digestion process.

Chapter Eight

Counting and Examples of Basal Metabolism

Simply put, metabolism covers everything that goes on inside the body to build and maintain tissues, produce energy, and make sure the body remains healthy. Basal metabolism can be described as the basic or least amount of energy needed for the body to survive and keep functioning during rest.

It doesn't include the extra energy that's needed to support the smallest amount of activity once the individual is awake and on the move.

If you're still not sure what basal metabolism has to do with anything, just think of it as the number of calories the body burns to get energy even while you're sleeping. The energy acquired is used for supporting the essential life functions like breathing, maintaining body temperature, to the pumping of blood in the system.

The body needs all the energy it can get to ensure you have the right amount of essential fluids and substances for metabolism. Let's take, for example, the nerves and muscles; they can't work sufficiently without a precise concentration of sodium and potassium. According to studies carried out, regulating and monitoring these minerals takes up about 20-40% of the body's resting energy.

Factors Influencing Basal Metabolism (BM)

There are tons of factors that affect people's basal metabolism. Some might have higher rates due to their genes, while some aren't so lucky and have lower ones. The BMR of men tends to be faster than that of women.

Muscle Mass

Since the muscles burn three times more calories than fat – even during sleep, it's safe to say that the proportion of muscle to fat changes the metabolic rate. The muscles require more energy to function than fatty tissues.

The more muscle tissue an individual has, the more energy their body needs to function correctly.

Age

The body loses muscle mass while aging, and this, in turn, slows down metabolism. Not consuming the right amount of calories to support the body's minimum energy needs will slow it down by 30% or more.

During development, growing children go through periods of growth that results in extreme metabolism rates.

Fever

Developing a fever tends to increase the body's metabolic rate by around 7% for every 0.5^0 Centigrade over the standard temperature. The metabolic rate could also drop by 30-40% if the thyroid gland fails to produce the right quantity of hormones.

Size

People with bigger bodies tend to have larger basal metabolic rates because their organs are larger, and there's an increased volume of fluids to maintain.

Environmental Factors

Changes to the environment like increased heat or cold could force the body into working harder to maintain its average temperature. This particular act leads to an increased basal metabolic rate.

Drugs

Substances such as caffeine and nicotine can increase the BMR of an individual, just as steroids and antidepressants can lead to weight gain regardless of their eating habits.

Diet

What you consume and how you eat it has a significant influence on your metabolic rate. It's no secret that food changes metabolism. The best thing to do is to watch what goes into your body.

Basal Metabolic Rate (BMR)

You can easily calculate your BMR by using the simple formula based on weight, height, and age; although, this style only provides you with an estimate.

Obtaining something more precise requires you considering all your factors, using special equipment, and acquiring results under the strictest possible condition. The BMR only accounts for around 70% of the used calories.

The total amount of energy burned is determined by your BMR + your physical activity level and the burned calories derived when digesting food and absorbing nutrients.

Understanding how the basal metabolism works provide you with a valuable tool demonstrating how you can influence metabolic rate through muscle mass and the right diet. A controlled diet tells your body when it needs to conserve calories and slow down metabolism.

Chapter Nine

Considering Macro and Micronutrients

Everyone and everything (plants, animals, and humans) require nutrients to survive and grow. Just as their names suggest, micronutrients are needed in small quantities while macronutrients are required in larger ones by the body.

We need them to survive, and these nutrients can be gotten from various diets and supplements that we consume daily. Even though micro and macronutrients can be acquired from the same source, they're relatively different from each other, in that they have separate uses and benefits.

Characteristics of Macronutrients

What are macronutrients? Simply put, they are known as essential compounds that the body doesn't supply or make in a sufficient capacity; as a result, external sources are needed to make up for it.

The human body needs large quantities of macronutrients to ensure that it functions at maximum optimum capacity. Most carbohydrates constitute these nutrients and as a result, are often eaten in large amounts. Carbs have high fiber contents which are necessary for promoting human growth.

Unlike micronutrients, macronutrients are essential for specifically enhancing growth. Fats, proteins, and carbs are typical examples of macronutrients and how they help in providing various areas of the body (brain, heart, kidneys, etc.) with energy to sustain normal functions.

Insufficient energy due to consuming little macronutrients often leads to fatigue and eventual shutdown of the body. The major types of foods that have a high content of macronutrients include; fish, meat, cereals, potatoes, oilseed, nuts, and yams, among other things.

Since most individuals undergoing the keto vegan diet can't eat most of the food items in the above category, they have to increase the amounts of the ones they're allowed to consume. So, that means more plant-based proteins and fats. Luckily, most plant-based foods are rich macronutrients

While lots of people might believe carbs hold center stage when it comes to macros, it's actually fats that take the throne. They're great for maintaining great health. Incorporating natural and healthy sources of fats like nuts, seeds, avocados, and coconut oil into our diets goes a long way in making us healthy.

Excessive consumption of macros in the form of carbs and saturated fats could eventually lead to health issues like diabetes or obesity. It goes without saying that while macronutrients are essential for the proper functioning of the body, they should be consumed in comparable levels to ensure optimum health.

Micronutrient Characteristics

They're required in small quantities by the body because it already makes most of the nutrients on its own. Most micronutrient sources come from minerals that exist in small quantities, making it challenging to consume in large amounts.

In contrast to macronutrients, micronutrients don't contain calories that provide energy to the body; instead, they have high volumes of antioxidants.

These minerals play a huge role in protecting the body from different kinds of diseases that might plague it.

Micronutrients also help in eliminating toxins that negatively impacts the

health of humans. They're pivotal in creating enzymes and some other components that aid in improving the various functions of the body.

Micronutrient examples include vitamins and minerals that are generally needed in small quantities by the body. Fruits and green leafy vegetables are among the examples of foods rich in micronutrients.

Studies show excessive consumption of micronutrients doesn't necessarily have adverse effects; although their deficiencies could lead to damaging impacts on health. Some of the problems they cause include; poor vision, constant fatigue, or several mental-related defects.

Differences between Macro and Micronutrients

Macronutrients	Micronutrients
Quantity:	
They're required in massive amounts to ensure optimal body performance and health.	The human body needs them in smaller quantities.
They're mostly found in large quantities in various kinds of food items which is	And they exist in smaller amounts in most food sources.

72

why they're needed in high amounts.

Body Functions:

Macros mostly provide the body with the energy it needs to carry out different activities and tasks.

They're responsible for body functions like; energy storage, repairing body tissues, maintaining an average temperature, promoting healthy function of cells and blood clotting, etc.

Micros promote muscle growth and improve the health of the body by preventing diseases from attacking it.

They support the healthy growth of the hair and skin cells, strong teeth, and bones, and produce hormones that enhances a great immune system.

Examples:

Fats, proteins, and carbs.

Vitamins and minerals (fruits and veggies).

Health Effects:

Excessive consumption could lead to obesity, which could be detrimental to health.

The excessive intake of micronutrients doesn't have any recorded side effects.

Insufficient amounts of macronutrients

Insufficient consumption of

73

consumed could result in malnutrition or kwashiorkor. micronutrients could result in deficiencies in the body (e.g., scurvy and goiter).

In everything that we do, it's always necessary to ensure a proper balance is struck to make sure optimum health is attained.

Protein Requirements

During the vegan keto diet, the consumption of protein is quite essential. While eating too much of it could be counterproductive in achieving ketosis since the body would have to store the excess amounts into glucose, consuming too little could lead to the breakdown of muscles and tissues. The key here is to strike the right balance between too much and too little and find a middle ground.

Let's take for example;

An individual weighing 160lb should consume about 1g of protein per kilogram of his/her body weight (BW). To calculate their BW in Kg, divide by 2.2lb/kg.

The daily protein requirement of a 160lb individual = 160/2.2 = 73kg.

This amount is pretty much adequate for relatively inactive people. But the ones looking to put on more weight and muscles, and are quite active should increase their number to between 100-120 grams during training days.

Getting Sufficient Amounts of Protein on the Keto Vegan Diet

The main challenge most keto-vegans face is finding the right plant-based proteins that hit the required numbers and aren't high in carbohydrates. What's most important is making sure you accumulate enough protein from vegan sources without allowing your carbohydrate-levels to spike.

If you'd instead get more protein from supplements, hemp and other sources of vegan protein powders (like rice and pea) are the best choices for athletes and gym enthusiasts. Those protein shakes tend to contain a 5:1 protein-to-carbohydrate ratio.

To avoid suffering from deficiencies, you'll need to find the best plant proteins that are both usable by your body and also count toward your goals. They need to support the muscle cells and general performance of the body without having to resort to meat or dairy products.

Right from time vegans have always known they can't get all the amino acids they need from a particular source of plant protein. That's why they make an effort to eat from diverse selections and combine several foods to make it up.

How to Fix Some Common Keto Vegan Deficiencies

During the ketogenic diet, we get to banish nearly all carbs from our lives and stick with high-fats. Being a vegan means no animal products; which just leaves us with less wiggle room to get a sufficient amount of essential nutrients needed for long-term health.

Most plant-based foods don't always provide the body with adequate nutrients needed. Some of them include;

Vitamin B12 (Cobalamin)

B12 is vital for the nervous system, skin, eyes, and hair cells. It aids in the digestion of fats, proteins, and carbohydrates. Unfortunately, this vitamin is a little bit hard to come by in some plant food items.

You can get a reasonably decent amount of B12 in some lower-carb sources like fortified almond milk, nutritional yeast, and nori (purple seaweed). Studies show that most plant-based foods that contain Vit B12 pack lots of carbs in them, so it's suggested you get the vitamin through vegan supplements. Look for the ones that provide about 6-10mcg of methyl-cobalamin (another form of Vit B12), because they're unlike cyanocobalamin which gets absorbed more easily.

Iron

It serves as a critical component of hemoglobin, which is responsible for transporting oxygen from the lungs to various parts of the body. Energy and vitality take a nosedive when iron and hemoglobin levels drop. The individual suffering from iron deficiency tends to appear weak and pale; with hairs and nails turning brittle and weak.

Vegetable-sourced iron (non-heme iron) is a lot harder to absorb than the ones found in animal products (heme iron). It's probably why this nutrient level still plummets even when dieters consume tons of iron-rich items like nuts, seeds, or Swiss chard.

It's recommended that you add a vegan-based iron supplement to your meal plan to complement the one you get from the vegetables. It's especially crucial for women to increase their consumption of the nutrient since they lose iron every month during menstruation.

EPA and DHA (Omega-3 fatty acids)

These fats provide the body with cellular building block structures that aid in preventing cardiovascular diseases. While fish oil is one of the most common sources of EPA and DHA, there are a few vegan alternatives that are just as good – if not better.

Algae offer a better concentration of DHA since it's where the fishes get their supply of Omega-3 when they eat it. Replacing fish with algae oil allows you to effectively cut out the middle man (the fish) and get the full nutritional content of the food. Try aiming for around 300mg of the oil daily.

Chapter Ten

Setting up the Keto Vegan Diet in a Correct and Lasting Way

Starting a keto vegan diet might seem pretty enough; I mean it's just eating lots of fatty foods right. Unfortunately, it takes more than that. You need to plan the entire process in the correct way so that you'd be able to enjoy more of the benefits of the diet, and less of the side effects.

Everyone's body has different needs, and the things that work for one person might not work for the next. So, you just have to figure out the best route to take when starting the diet.

Laying a Proper Groundwork

One of the greatest benefits of the keto vegan diet is metabolic flexibility. The ability of the body to pull energy both from the glucose and ketones produced makes it metabolically flexible; giving it benefits that extend all through the system.

Also, eliminating sugar and high levels of carbohydrates from the diet makes it possible for the body to heal and detoxify itself from the accumulated inflammations.

Before rushing into the vegan diet (maybe because everyone around is doing it) try laying the groundwork for it. What this means is that you need to try lowering your carb intake to fewer than 20g for at least 2-3 weeks for your body to become adapted to the idea of keto.

Once you're successful at that, you'd be able to go in and out of ketosis without suffering from whiplash. You'd be able to reap the benefits that accompany not being glucose-dependent.

Common Mistakes People Make on the Diet

- **Stuffing themselves with fat bombs:** Lots of individuals think that the best way to get their macronutrient ratios in line is by loading up on highly concentrated fatty foods. You don't necessarily have to put extra fat on every meal or even in your coffee just because you want to make it high-fat. It's overkill.

   It might be an excellent strategy for when you're still transitioning from the glucose-dependent diet, but once you've adapted, it's not necessary. Along the way, learn to pay attention to your body's hunger cues, as this would make you an intuitive eater. If you catch yourself feeling hungry shortly after a meal, then it's most likely you didn't consume enough fats or protein.

   You'll find that when you're satiated and full, there won't be much reason for you to consume excessive amounts of fat.

- **Chasing blood ketones:** Rather than focusing on hormone signals, some people focus more on the ketones in their blood. A higher amount of ketones in the urine means you have more ketone bodies circulating in your bloodstream. But it doesn't mean you're doing a great job of burning fat for fuel. The only way to know if the diet is working for sure is when you attain nutritional ketosis (being between 1.5 – 3.0mol/L on the ketone meter). Hormone signals let you know when you are fat-adapted – not the quantity of ketones on the blood meter.

- **Remaining in Ketosis for long:** Unless you have a medical condition (like epilepsy) that needs you to remain in ketosis for long periods at a time, it's recommended you don't stay in the state for too long. Chronic ketosis tends to cause muscle soreness, fatigue, nausea, and insomnia. And if you're just starting, professionals recommend that you go through the adaptation phase, so your body gets used to burning both fats and glucose for fuel.

Transitioning to the Vegan Keto Diet the Right Way

Depending on your current metabolic state, reprogramming your body to switch from burning glucose to fats could take anywhere from 2-6 weeks. Unless your diet was already clean to start with or you were into Paleo, it could be difficult jumping into this new style of eating without preamble.

Like with every journey, proper preparation is needed to get you into the keto spirit. You need to start small first and change your mindset that this is just another diet; it's not. If you're used to consuming large amounts of highly-processed carbs and sugary foods, you'll need to ease yourself into the diet.

The first step should be eliminating refined sugars, carbs, artificial, and processed food from your meal plan. It doesn't mean you have to stay away from your favorite foods forever. Once you're done with the adaptation phase, and you attain ketosis, you can begin experimenting with the various keto versions of your favorites.

Another vital thing to consider when starting a keto vegan diet is to test your blood ketones while monitoring your carb intake. If you don't do so, it would be difficult for you to know if you've genuinely attained keto-adaptation.

The fat-adaptation phase tends to be the most difficult as your body tries to get used to the new changes. Be sure to expect fatigue, headaches, and some form of withdrawal (for some). Always remember to take it easy and slow.

Tips to Follow

If you're already on the vegan keto diet and things are working out for you, then keep doing what you're doing. But if you don't always feel too good or suffer from way too many side effects, you need to stop and re-evaluate your tactics.

1. **Make sure you listen to your body:** Your body will always send you signals on how to react to certain situations and signals. It's your job to listen to it and tailor your diet accordingly.

2. **Cycle in and out of ketosis:** Allow your body to adapt to the new situation by getting in and out of the vegan keto diet. Giving your body little breaks allow you to train it to be flexible as to what fuel source it burns.

3. **Change some of your lifestyle choices:** To get the maximum benefits of the diet, it's essential to stick to a health plan which includes staying hydrated, exercising regularly, and getting adequate sleep. Get rid of your bad habits, like overeating high-carbs and consuming tons of alcohol.

4. **Upgrade your nutrient quality:** Even though the vegan diet is already healthier than the non-vegan ones, there might still be some things you can improve in your diet. Eat fewer carbs, a moderate amount of proteins, and more essential fatty acids.

5. **Get enough salts (sodium, magnesium, and potassium):** Because we typically consume large amounts of processed foods, we naturally get enough sodium in our regular diet. But when most people start the keto diet, they have to cut out these kinds of foods.

   It's easy to think of low sodium levels as not much of a problem, but it tends to cause fatigue and cravings; which is why we need sufficient amounts in our diets. Individuals on the vegan keto diet tend to excrete large amounts of potassium, making it necessary to replenish the source; especially if you're active. Spinach and avocados are excellent sources of the nutrient.

6. **Don't cut out exercise from your routine:** It might be mentally draining to continue exercising while starting the keto vegan diet; especially the first few weeks. However, it's good to try doing some exercises if you can manage it since it helps your body get adapted to the diet a lot faster (plus you'll lose fats instead of muscle during the process).

   Start small by taking long walks (since it's the most straightforward option) or doing small exercises like sit-ups, pushups, or squats at home.

Getting into Ketosis on the Vegan Keto Diet

Most times, just restricting carb content to low levels results in ketosis. Other factors play major roles, but sticking to a low-carb diet is essential. Restrict carbohydrates to 20g or less each day. You don't need to restrict fiber since it's beneficial to ketosis.

Limit proteins to moderate levels. The ketogenic diet doesn't need much protein to function; although the quantity is more than that of carbohydrates. Just like with carbs, excess proteins are converted in the body to glucose, which reduces ketosis. One of the common mistakes people make when trying to enter ketosis is consuming too many proteins. Try aiming to eat only the protein you need at a particular time; nothing more.

Unlike starving to achieve ketosis, the high-fat diet is sustainable. Starvation causes the individual to feel exhausted and weak, but the keto diet allows you to feel great. The key to a successful low-carb diet is eating enough fat until you feel satisfied. And if you're feeling hungry all the time, it means you need to increase the amount of fatty foods in your diet.

Avoid unnecessary snacking as this slows down ketosis and reduces weight loss. Keto-friendly snacks tend to minimize the damage, though. So, if you must eat something besides the regular meal, you could try the keto vegan snack option.

If you feel you can handle it, try intermittent fasting as it's effective at boosting ketone levels, reversing Type-II diabetes, and accelerating weight loss. Consider skipping breakfast and only eating for eight hours a day and fasting for sixteen (16:8).

Add exercise to the mix even though it might not be essential to achieve ketosis; it's useful for increasing ketone levels at a moderate rate. It's also advisable to keep fit just for the sake of looking and feeling good.

While dieting, it's crucial that you get enough sleep. For most people, an average of seven hours every night works fine for them. Adequate sleep is vital for keeping stress levels under control. Sleep deprivation leads the stress hormones to spike, which in turn leads to increased blood sugar levels, which slow ketosis and weight loss.

Ways of Knowing you're in Ketosis

It's possible to measure ketone levels by testing urine, breath, or blood samples. Other than that, other telltale signs reveal when you're in ketosis.

- **Keto Breath:** This usually happens due to the acetone escaping from our breaths. Attaining ketosis makes the breath to develop a particular "fruity" smell (similar to nail polish remover). The smell is often temporary and can be felt sometimes from sweat during workout sessions.
- **Dry Mouth:** Undergoing the diet might sometimes lead to an increased urge to drink water. So, unless you already drink a lot, or get sufficient electrolytes, (like salt), you'll experience the sensation of dry mouth. To get the metallic taste out of the mouth, try drinking as much water as possible.
- **Increase in urination:** Due to the dry mouth and increased thirst, urine production increases during ketosis.

- **Fewer Hunger Pangs:** While on the keto diet, lots of people experience a noticeable reduction in hunger. It might be caused by the body using its fat stores as fuel. Most of them end up feeling great when they eat just once or twice a day.

- **A possible increase in energy:** After the initial exhaustion, individuals feel as a result of the keto flu, a marked increase in energy levels is experienced later — some credit the sensation as a sense of euphoria or lack of brain fog.

How to Measure Ketosis

There are three main ways of measuring ketones in the body after starting the diet. The different methods all have their fair share of pros and cons, so it's up to you to decide which one works best for your situation.

Using the Urine Strip

This urinalysis test method is usually the first method beginners use since it is simple and quite affordable. In this method, ketosis is measured using strips.

All you need to do is get the strip and dip it in your urine (works best with the first urine of the day) and wait for fifteen seconds for the color to change and reveal the presence of ketones. If you notice a dark purple color on the stick (which means a high reading), just know you're in ketosis.

Pros

The advantage of this test method is that the strips are available almost everywhere (pharmacies and even Amazon) and reasonably priced. A very strong-positive test can reliably prove to you that you're in ketosis.

Cons

The results of the strip could vary depending on how much fluids you consume daily. The more amount of water you drink, the more you dilute the concentrations of the ketones in the urine. And as a result, the strip would only be able to detect lower levels of the ketone bodies.

This method isn't always accurate since there are several factors to consider first. Also, as you proceed on the keto vegan diet and your body becomes increasingly keto-adapted, it reabsorbs the ketones back from the urine; making the strip unreliable in detecting ketosis. The ketones remain more in the bloodstream instead of getting lost through excretion.

The lack of ketone bodies in the urine could lead the test strip to produce a false negative result even when you've been in ketosis for weeks.

Using the Breath Analyzers

The breath-ketone analyzer (breathalyzer) is quite simple to use as it measures the ketones in your breath. They're more expensive than the urine strips, but still cheaper than the third option (we'll get to that shortly) since they can be used several times.

Even though these analyzers don't provide an accurate ketone level when used on its own, they often offer a color code to depict the general levels.

It's also possible to hook up the device to a computer or smartphone to get more precise ketone numbers through the app.

Pro

The test is relatively simple to carry out, and, it can be done multiple times.

Cons

It doesn't always relate well with blood ketones and isn't always accurate. And sometimes the values gotten from the device could be entirely misleading. Assuming you recently consumed pizza which is high in carbs, the result you'll get on the breathalyzer will be off since your breath integrity has been compromised.

Using the Blood-Ketone Meters

These gadgets show the current and exact ketone levels in the bloodstream. They're the most accurate way to measure ketosis while on the keto vegan diet.

Pros

They're reliable and offer accurate readings.

Cons

The tests are pretty expensive to carry out (at least one dollar per test), and they require drawing blood from the finger. Even though only a prick on the finger is required, some people dread the thought of sticking a needle in themselves.

How to Achieve Optimal Ketosis

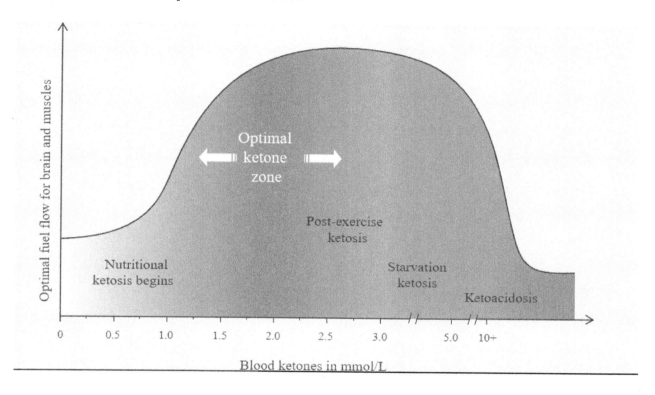

Being in a state of ketosis isn't exactly a 'yes' or 'no' thing. Some people believe that you're either ketosis or you're not, but that's not the case here. There are different levels or degrees of ketosis.

o **Less than 0.5mmol/l**: Anything below this value isn't considered ketosis. It means you're on your way there, but you still have a long way to go before reaching maximum fat-burning.

o **From 0.5 – 1.5mmol/l:** This range shows you've arrived at light nutritional ketosis. It'll likely have a good impact on your weight, but not much.

- **Around 1.5 – 3mmol/l**: This range is known as optimal ketosis, and it's usually recommended for maximum physical and mental performance. Fat burning and increased weight loss are maximized in this state.

- **Over 3mmol/l:** These levels tend to be higher than necessary and will probably not give you better or worse results than what you'd get from the 1.5 – 3 level. In some cases, higher numbers could mean you aren't getting enough food. Anything over 3mmol/l is dubbed "starvation ketosis."

- **Between 8 – 10mmol/l:** Normally, it's impossible to reach this level by just consuming a keto vegan diet. Anything more than 8 – 10mmol/l is an indication that something is wrong. One of the main causes of this is type 1 diabetes. The patients tend to suffer from a severe lack of insulin. The possible end-result (ketoacidosis) could be fatal and requires urgent medical care.

You don't necessarily have to reach optimal ketosis to start experiencing weight loss benefits. From 0.5mmol/l and above reveal those benefits. But, you might need to achieve higher levels to attain high-level physical performances.

You don't have to rush the process; allow your body to adapt. It might take weeks or even a couple of months for all the benefits of the keto vegan diet to start rolling in.

Chapter Eleven

Difficulties that Arise during the Diet

So, at this point, you've probably already begun your keto vegan journey. And by now you've most likely run into some of the obstacles that make the entire thing almost tedious. It's normal to encounter difficulties along the way; nothing good tends to come easy.

You might find it difficult starting the vegan keto diet, especially since your body needs to adjust to the new normal (at least for the period you'll spend on the diet).

Most times, the problems you might be facing could be easily solved by increasing your water and salt intake; although not every challenge is as easy as that. And when you do this, you'll find that your problems might reduce considerably.

Here are some notable side effects of the diet and their possible solution;

Induction (Keto) Flu

When most individuals start the high-fat low-carb diet, one of the first issues they experience is the keto flu (as it's popularly called). It occurs within the first week – around day 2-4.

The term flu comes from the fact that the ailment mimics flu-like symptoms. During this transition period, it's normal to feel tired, lethargic, headaches, nausea, and lack of motivation or 'brain fog.' Some people even feel irritated by anyone in their immediate vicinity.

The good about these symptoms is that they don't usually last for long and disappear on their own after a few days. It's also possible to avoid them altogether by staying hydrated and consuming more sodium. You could easily add a half teaspoon of salt to a large cup of water and drink it. Repeating this practice would help you feel less miserable when you start experiencing these symptoms.

Leg Cramps

This side effect isn't uncommon for individuals beginning any strict low-carb diet. The issue might seem minor at first, but it can be painful to deal with for some. Leg cramps occur as a result of the loss of minerals (especially magnesium) through increased urination.

The best way to handle the situation is by drinking lots of fluid and salt; if needed, get magnesium supplements for the time being. But if neither options work, you might want to consider increasing your carb consumption by a little bit; although this might affect your diet.

Constipation

Having difficulty stooling is another effect of the low-carb diet – especially during the first week. Your digestive system is taking the time to adapt to its new situation, and as a result, it becomes increasingly difficult to get rid of wastes.

As usual, drinking lots of water and salt tends to ease the problem. Also, you need to get a good source of quality fiber to consume since most of the previous options involved high-carbs. Eat plenty of non-starchy vegetables or dissolve psyllium seed husks to a glass of water and drink it.

Bad Breath

While on the keto vegan diet, there's a high chance that your breath would start smelling different. The almost fruity smell comes from acetone – a ketone body, and it's a sure sign that your body is already burning tons of fats and converting them to ketones as fuel.

However, not everyone on the keto diet experiences the lousy breath effect. For some people, it manifests in their sweat, especially when they work out too much. The good news here is that this side effect doesn't last long (a week or two). Once the body adapts to the fat, it stops leaking ketones through the sweat and breath.

On the off-chance that the bad breath doesn't go away (yes, it's been known to happen once in a while), here are several ways to remedy the issue.

  i.   Drink lots of fluids
 ii.   Practice good oral hygiene (brush maybe thrice a day)
iii.   Get a breath-freshener to mask the smell
 iv.   Wait and see if it's temporary (most times it is)
  v.   Slightly reduce the degree of your ketosis by eating a bit more carbs (it shouldn't stop your progress though)

Increased Heart Rate

It's not surprising to experience heart palpitations during the first couple of weeks on the low-carb diet. It shows your heart is beating harder – which isn't abnormal. It means there's a reduction of circulating fluid in the bloodstream and your heart is working harder to pump more blood to maintain the pressure.

As usual, drinking more fluids help ease this symptom. The increased heart pumping could also be because of the new changes to the body and the stress it has to endure. But, if you already have previous cardiac issues, you might need to consult your physician for more information on the situation.

Reduction in Physical Performance

During the initial weeks of starting the keto vegan diet, your physical performance might be severely reduced mostly due to fat-adaptation and lack of fluids and salts.

The fat-adaptation process might take a little time for the body to adjust, but it can be improved by exercising more during the diet. The benefits of the low-carb, high-fat diet can be seen most times in long-distance races and other sports that require pushing your endurance levels.

This happens because the body's fat stores are a lot greater than the glycogen ones. It shows once the body becomes fat-adapted, athletes could perform for more extended periods without the need for external energy. As they exercise, their body uses up the fat as fuel.

It frees them from having to activate their gastrointestinal organs during the activity, and a large portion of blood flow would be directed to the muscles. Plus, a low-carb diet comes with a reduction of body fats which allows the athletes to feel lighter; increasing their output.

Temporary Loss of Hair

This symptom could occur in pretty much any major diet change, and it happens for different reasons, none of which is permanent. It's common in low-carb diets because of the restriction of calories.

Fortunately, the hair loss doesn't happen to everyone and is barely noticeable with people that experience it. Naturally, individuals already experience little amounts of hair loss when new hair follicles push the old ones out – but we don't notice it since it's infinitesimal.

When the body starts going through stress, more strands are lost than usual due to numerous reasons all having to do with the diet. There's really not much to do about this symptom than eating nutritious veggies and sleeping well since the effects are temporary. Also, try to reduce other external sources of stress to the body.

Elevated Cholesterol

The great news about the keto vegan diet is that it leads to an improved cholesterol profile, resulting in a lower risk of cardiac diseases. One of the positive effects is it elevates HDL reduces signs of atherosclerosis.

Even though it's rare, very few people (partly due to genetics) still end up with high elevations of LDL and total cholesterol; none of which could be considered normal. This potential risk can be taken care of through little steps like;

- **Avoid drinking bulletproof coffee:**

This brand of beverage involves adding MCT oil, butter, or coconut fat to coffee. Don't consume significant amounts of fatty drinks when you're not hungry. It'll play a vital role in normalizing your cholesterol levels

- **Use more unsaturated fats (avocados, olive oil)**

It'll go a long way in lowering your already high cholesterol.

- **Eat only when you're hungry**

Intermittently fasting once in a while should help in reducing your levels

- And if nothing else works for you, consider looking for a less strict diet.

Low-Carb and Alcohol Intolerance

Most people on low-carb diets tend to lose their tolerance for alcohol and get intoxicated quickly. That's why you need to be careful when drinking alcohol on a low-carb diet. You could always think of it as a way of saving money at the bar since you only need half as many drinks to get a buzz going.

There's no apparent cut reason yet for this phenomenon. It could be that the liver is too busy producing ketones to have the time or capacity to burn the alcohol you're consuming.

Or it could be that sugar (fructose) and alcohol are almost similarly broken down in the liver, and consuming a reduced quantity could make the liver briefly less adapted to breaking down the alcohol.

Regardless of what the science behind the process is, the fact is that keto diet reduces your tolerance for alcohol. So, always remember to be careful if you decide to drink.

Period Changes

While on the keto diet, some women might notice a change in their menstrual cycle. In some cases, it becomes irregular, while in some others it stops altogether. This situation occurs mostly due to rapid weight loss due to drops in gonadotropin-releasing hormone (GRH), estrogen, progesterone, luteinizing hormone (LH), and follicle-stimulating hormone (FSH).

When this disruption to the menstrual period occurs, serious side effects tend to follow, such as; low bone density, depression, anxiety, and sexual dysfunction. If your period suddenly becomes irregular or stops entirely during this diet, you need to consult your doctor as soon as possible because it's a bad sign.

However, there's a plus side to this for women with polycystic ovary syndrome (PCOS). It's a loophole of sorts. The keto diet helps people suffering from PCOS in regulating their periods.

Whether you have any preexisting health issues, it's best to ask your physician if it's okay for you to embark on the keto vegan diet since they're so many things to consider. If you suffer from any type of kidney dysfunction, Type-1 or 2 Diabetes, or a heart defect, you might want to avoid the diet or get approval from your doctor first.

Ketosis is actually beneficial to individuals suffering from hyperglycemia issues; although they have to be careful of their blood sugar and check their glucose levels multiple times daily.

Reasons Why You Might not be Losing Weight on the Keto Vegan Diet

There are so many possible reasons why you're not shedding pounds even

after spending weeks doing the keto diet, and you're following the guidelines. Before you decide to give up and go back to your carbs and bread, consider these following explanations.

1) You probably never entered ketosis

This idea might seem crazy to you, especially when you've spent all these while slashing your carb levels and curbing your sweet tooth. But if you can't see any visible results after spending so long on the diet, then you need to make sure that you're doing the right thing. So, hit the pause button and test your urine or blood to see if there's ketone in your bloodstream. And if it turns out that you're not in ketosis, try increasing your daily fat content from 75% to around 90% for better results.

2) You're consuming more proteins than necessary

The keto vegan diet is high-fat and not high-protein; try not to mistake the two things. As a result, you need a moderate amount of proteins and more fatty foods. Consuming high amounts of proteinic food could prevent you from achieving ketosis – or even kick you out of it if you're already there.

3) You're probably missing hidden carb sources

Vegetables and nuts are keto-friendly, and all, but some of them contain high amounts of carbs. If you don't pay enough attention to the contents of most of the food you eat, you will end up surpassing your daily carb content. You need to limit your daily carbohydrate calories to 2-5%, which means you need to keep track of almost every single bite. No one said this diet would be easy.

4) High daily calorie intake

Regardless of which nutrient group you're getting your calories from, once it's higher than what your body needs at a particular time, the rest is stored as fat. And that means you'll gain weight even if you're in ketosis.

If you want your diet to become successful, you need to pay close attention to everything you eat and do. It's crucial because one misstep could affect your entire result.

Debunking Some Common Keto Vegan Myths

Despite the apparent benefits of the diet, there's still some air of uncertainty around it. Some people don't feel assured of the merits of following a high-fat, low-carb meal plan, especially when it combines veganism to the mix. They think it limits their already slim food-pool.

Let's take a look at the top four myths;

#1: Eating lots of Fatty Foods makes you Fat

This common misconception is probably popular due to years of marketing of low-fat products to consumers. Most health ads and commercial feature greasy burgers and grease as a way of deterring people from consuming foods containing high fats.

When in actuality, the problem originates from meals laden with high amounts of carbohydrates and processed sugar. They cause most of the health complications that are linked with diabetes and other diseases.

As soon as you kick your unhealthy habits and stick to a quality high-fat diet that includes avocados, nuts, and vegetables, your body will stop storing excessive amounts of glucose used as body fat. And unlike with a high-carb diet, eating healthy fatty foods keep you satisfied and curb your cravings. Once your appetite is suppressed, you'll be less likely to consume so many calories.

#2: The diet won't be sustaining since it's deficient in some vitamins and minerals

If you follow the keto vegan diet correctly, it contains all the essential micronutrients your body needs to function correctly. Some people might wonder how possible it is to skip some fruits (oranges and apples) and still remain healthy.

It's easy since there are several low-carb vegetables (spinach, arugula, and berries) that offer all the essential vitamins and minerals you get from those particular fruits; minus the sugar.

#3: As long as you keep your carb levels low, you can eat as much protein

As we mentioned earlier, consuming so many proteins is a common rookie misstep during the keto vegan diet. Excess amount of proteins in the body leads to gluconeogenesis, which causes it to convert the surplus amino acids to glucose. And this act prevents ketosis from happening. On the ketogenic diet, fat is the body's primary source of fuel. Remember that there's no such thing as 'essential carbs,' only 'essential fats.'

#4: The ketogenic diet causes electrolyte deficiency and dehydration

While this myth has a little bit of truth to it, there are still ways to avoid it from happening in the first place. The deficiency of electrolytes in the body is a pretty valid concern and can be remedied by drinking lots of water, salt, and taking supplements.

As long as you follow all the rules governing the keto vegan diet, you shouldn't encounter much difficulties achieving ketosis successfully. The process is long and sometimes challenging, but in the end, the results are worth the entire ordeal.

Chapter Twelve

Suggestions and Foods to Consider

There are so many food options to consider seeing as there are tons of vegetables in the world – even though we tend to eat a few particular ones. Let's take a look at some of the high-fat foods we're familiar with, and the ones we're not.

Avocados

This vegetable tends to work as both ingredients and a standalone meal. They're arguably the trendiest foods right now seeing as they work perfectly with almost everything. They can be used as toppings or fillers, cooking oil, or spreads for other meals. And they contain most, if not all, nutrients.

Berries

They work perfectly for the keto vegan diet because of their low sugar content. The berries include; blueberries, blackberries, blackberries, and strawberries, to name a few. These small glycemic berries tend to be slowly digested and absorbed; resulting in lower blood glucose.

Meat Substitutes

Tofu, tempeh, seitan, and several other vegan meat substitutes are often rich in proteins and low in carbs. Not only do they taste great, but these food options can also be cooked and presented in different forms (i.e., smoked tofu). It means you can still enjoy all your favorite dishes without using meat or poultry birds.

Carrots

These vegetables have higher carbohydrate content than their other leafy counterparts. You can still incorporate them into your meals; it just means you need to consume them in moderation while considering your daily carb intake. Carrots could serve as a substitute for hot dogs in individual dishes.

Peanut Butter

You can add them to various meal options or just slather them on a keto-vegan-friendly toast. Remember to check the content and nutritional facts of the brand you purchase before getting it. Also, avoid the ones with honey as part of its ingredients.

Cauliflower

Since the keto diet prevents you from eating most grains and cereals, cauliflower here serves as a great substitute. It can be prepared in various ways; from roasted cauliflower to grilled, seasoned, or baked. It could also work as a crust or filling for some keto vegan meals.

Pistachios

They're packed with vitamins and minerals and serve as great snacks. They're also low in calories and fat, which means you'll need to accompany them with other high-fat foods.

Leafy Greens

This category comprises of broccoli, kale, lettuce, spinach, and every other leafy green vegetable. They also have low calorie-content. And you can

consume them in massive quantities since they're packed with tons of essential nutrients and vitamins.

Zucchini

They're also known as 'zoodles' for their popular use as substitutes for noodles. This vegetable can be eaten in various forms. Individuals that want something crispy and crunchy could try the baked zucchini chips. They're great snacks; just remember to replace the breadcrumbs for dairy-free cheese.

Eggplants

They serve as great carb-replacers because they act as substitutes for most of the popular carbohydrate options like non-keto vegan pizzas or pasta. Eggplants also have numerous health benefits, which include reducing cholesterol levels and improving heart functions.

Mushrooms

They add spice to various keto vegan meal options such as the Shitake mushroom noodles and Sautéed Mushrooms. They are filled with antioxidants and are low in calories and fat-free.

Squash

These vegetables are fantastic for making soup, spaghetti, or even different roasted snacks. Squashes could be lifesavers, especially on days when you find yourself craving pasta or soup. Whatever form you decide to go for with this vegetable, be rest assured it's highly nutritive.

Yogurt Alternatives

Nuts like coconut milk or cashew nut serve as great substitutes for dairy-based yogurts. Not only do they satisfy your cravings, but you can also use for baking and for other meal options. Make sure to check the labels before purchase to ensure there isn't any sugar in it and the yogurt is both keto and vegan-friendly.

Meal Suggestions

Taco Stuffed Avocados

Move aside tortilla chips! Avocado is here to stay. This delicious keto and vegan meal is made of cauliflower rice, crushed walnuts, and other spices to make a low-carb taco filling. They're perfect for a light lunch and can be accompanied with sugar-free salsa.

Keto Mac and Cheese (Dairy-free)

Thanks to a genius, what was once believed to be a no-go area for keto vegan dieters because of the macaroni and cheese in it, has now been converted to

suit our low-carb needs. This version is a healthy substitute for America's popular comfort food. It's made from cauliflower and allows individuals to remain in ketosis and still have fun.

Mushroom Fried Rice Skillet

Once again, cauliflower plays a major role in recreating a delicious meal. It's filled with most of the best low-carb vegetables and is suitable for pretty much any cooking skillset. The mushroom fried rice can be enjoyed as either a main dish or a side one.

Thai Curry

Since it's naturally free from any animal product, curry tends to act as the best friend of most vegans. It can be made in just about any form without you getting bored. Most curries have complex flavors and are pretty easy to make.

Zucchini Noodles with Pesto

Zucchini is quite surprising seeing as there are tons of variations for it. The most popular form most dieters prefer is the noodle one – which can be created with the help of a spiralizer. The recipe is easy to make and helps in satisfying cravings for noodles.

Low-Carb Vegan Pizza Crust

There are tons of vegetarian pizzas out there, but unfortunately for vegans, they contain eggs. Thankfully, several recipes have popped up that don't require any animal product.

This low-carb coconut based pizza is the answer to the prayers of most vegans on the keto diet. And you can also pick out different low-carb toppings to go with the dish.

Cauliflower Steak with Lemon Tahini Dressing

Who says vegans can't have steaks too? Well, this vegan-friendly version uses herbed cauliflower as the alternative for meat. The lemon tahini dressing adds a fruity taste to the dish. You might feel like cauliflower has no business masquerading as steak, but once you taste it, you'll probably change your mind.

Avocado Fries

This snack-option serves as yet another way to enjoy avocado. Instead of going with potato fries (which are high-carbs), this fried avocado is both delicious and healthy. It's soft on the inside and crispy on the outside. It doesn't require many ingredients, and cooking takes less than twenty minutes.

Other delicious keto vegan meal suggestions include;

- Scrambled tofu
- Roasted cauliflower tofu tacos
- Vegan Almond Pancakes
- Lemon Garlic Roasted Asparagus
- Chocolate Almond Avocado Pudding
- Mashed Cauliflower with Garlic & Herbs
- Broccoli Fried Rice
- Tomato Mushroom Spaghetti Squash
- Avocado Tomato Arugula Salad
- Low-Carb Maple Oatmeal (minus the oats)
- Walnut Chili

- Broccoli Rice Tabbouleh
- Vegetable Soup
- Shirataki Noodles with Almond Butter Sauce

Being vegan and participating in a low-carb, high-fat diet is certainly no cakewalk, and can be incredibly stressful, but once you start the process, you'll see come to enjoy the lifestyle.

It doesn't need to be difficult coming up with options for your meal plans. All you need is a little imagination, and you're good to go.

Chapter Thirteen

Keto-Vegan Breakfast Recipes - Lunch Recipes - Dinner Recipes - Snack Recipes

There are tons of recipes for the keto vegan diet, which makes it easy to eat a variety of foods without having to repeat the same thing over and over again. Even the traditional non-vegan meals are being turned to favor dieters.

Here are a few easy-to-prepare recipes for the different mealtimes;

Breakfast

This is the most important meal of the day. The first item on the list is the vegan almond pancake, which is excellent for people who love the taste and feel of pancakes. This keto-vegan version is rich in fats and low on carbs; making it perfect for starting the day.

Vegan Almond Pancakes

Before we begin, it's essential to allow your batter to sit for a couple of minutes for the flax egg to assume a gel-like form, and the coconut flour to absorb the liquid. If you don't do any of these, the mixture won't work.

Make sure your batter is thick – not runny, and it shouldn't pour quickly unless it doesn't form the pancakes. If the mixture is too thin, you could always add a teaspoon or two of coconut flour.

If you don't have access to almond butter, there's the option of using peanut butter instead. Regardless, they both work out well for the batter. And if you don't want to add nuts, use sunflower seed butter. Use coconut cream and cinnamon as vegan butter substitutes to give your mixture a particular taste and texture.

This version of almond pancakes doesn't contain any sweetener, so if you want to make it sweeter, you should consider adding a little bit of liquid stevia or any granulated sweetener (about 1-2 tablespoons).

Ingredients

- Unsweetened almond milk (1/4 cups)
- Coconut flour (one tablespoon)
- Ground flax (one tablespoon)
- Unsweetened almond butter (two tablespoons)
- Baking powder (1/2 teaspoon)
- A pinch of salt (if the almond butter isn't salted already)
- Swerve or liquid stevia for extra taste (optional)

Preparation

Heat your frying pan or skillet on low-medium heat. Oil the pan with a little amount of keto-friendly oil; remember that it counts as part of your nutrition information.

Combine the almond milk and butter together in a small bowl. Get another dish and add the dry ingredients to it and mix until everything blends smoothly. Once you're done, combine both the wet and dry ingredients and stir until everything is blended properly.

Allow the mixture to sit for a little while (about 3-5 minutes) so that the coconut flour and flax can absorb the liquid effectively. Once it's done sitting, spoon the batter into your pan or skillet and gently spread into pancake forms and the size of your choice.

If the batter is proving challenging to spread, try wetting the back of the spoon and using like a spatula to move the dough. Allow the pancakes to cook for about 4-5 minutes or until they can be flipped easily.

You'll want to see tiny little bubbles all over the surface of the pancakes like with the regular ones. When the underside turns golden, flip it over and cook the other side for about 2-3 minutes until everything's done.

Once your pancakes are ready, bring them out and serve on plates with vegan butter, berries, almond butter, coconut cream, or sugar-free syrup as your topping. Regardless of the combo, you choose the pancakes will still be awesome to eat.

Vegan Almond Butter Pancakes

Nutrition Facts

Serving Size: 1 full recipe

Amount Per Serving		% Daily Value*
Calories	259.6 kcal	13 %
Total Fat	20.8 g	32 %
Saturated Fat	2.3 g	11 %
Trans Fat	0 g	
Cholesterol	0 mg	0 %
Sodium	59.8 mg	2 %
Total Carbohydrate	13.9 g	5 %
Dietary Fiber	8.8 g	35 %
Sugars	1.6 g	
Protein	9.6 g	19 %
Vitamin A	2 % • Vitamin C	0 %
Calcium	51 % • Iron	15 %

* Percent Daily Values are based on a 2,000 calorie diet. Your daily values may be higher or lower depending on your calorie needs.

Full Info at cronometer.com

Peanut Butter Chia Pudding

This healthy keto vegan breakfast option is made up of chia seeds, sugar-free monk fruit syrup, and almond milk (unsweetened one).

Ingredients

- Vanilla essence (one teaspoon)
- Ground chia seeds (27g ¼ cup)
- Sea salt (1/4 teaspoon)
- One cup of peanut butter (no added sugar or oil)
- Unsweetened almond milk ($1^1/_4$ cups)
- Sugar-free maple flavored syrup (1/4 cup)
- 2-3 drops of pure monk fruit extract (if the batter isn't sweet enough for you)

Ingredients for Toppings

- Peanut butter (one teaspoon)
- Crushed peanuts (1/2 teaspoon)
- One teaspoon of dark chocolate chunks (sugar-free or 85% cocoa)
- One teaspoon of melted dark chocolate (sugar-free or 85% cocoa)

Preparations

Add all the ingredients into a blender – not minding the order. Blend the contents for thirty seconds or less, stop and scrape the bottom and sides with a spatula to mix everything together. Continue blending again for up to a minute or until the mixture becomes smooth and creamy.

Try checking the sweetness (or lack of) at this point and make necessary adjustments when needed. You could add more drops of the monk fruit extract (or stevia) to make the sweeter.

If you use maple-flavored syrup, it could end up changing the texture of the pudding; making it more liquid than thick. If that happens, you might want to stick with the drops of monk fruit extract.

As soon as you're done blending, transfer the contents into small jars or containers, and refrigerate for three hours or more to get the best flavor and creamy texture.

Serve the pudding with any topping you choose. The sugar-free chocolate chunks, crushed peanuts, and a drizzle of peanut butter should go smoothly with your chia pudding. You could either serve the meal as breakfast or dessert; it works either way.

Scrambled Vegan Tofu

Ingredients

- Extra-firm Tofu (~220g, 8 ounces)
- Paprika (1/2 teaspoon)
- Turmeric (1/2 teaspoon)
- Garlic Powder (1/2 teaspoon)
- Onion Powder (1/4 teaspoon)
- Vegan Butter (one tablespoon)
- Dijon Mustard (one teaspoon)
- Soy milk 80ml (1/3 cup)
- Nutritional Yeast (two tablespoons)
- ¼ teaspoon of Black Salt (Kala Namak provides an eggy flavor)

You could also consider adding chopped chives, fried tomatoes, black pepper, and sliced avocado when you serve the meal. Not only do they give the food a fantastic appearance, but they're also quite healthy too.

Preparations

Use a fork to mash the tofu. But don't smash everything completely; leave some big chunks. Get a large bowl and add the turmeric, yeast, Dijon mustard, paprika, black salt, onion, and garlic powder to it. Add your soy milk to the ingredients and whisk them up to give you a sweet sauce.

Place the vegan butter in a frying pan or skillet and heat until it's hot. Then add the tofu; frying it until it turns light brown. Try as much as possible not to break it up when moving the tofu around the pan while cooking.

Add your sauce to the pan and continue frying until you achieve the desired state. You can have the tofu as wet or as dry as you like since it will absorb the sauce in the pan. When you're done, slice some black peppers, chopped chives, avocados, and fried tomatoes, and use as toppings for your scrambled tofu.

Side Note

If you can't find the black salt, you could always use the regular one; although it's recommended that you try and look for it since the regular salt won't give you the eggy flavor that the black one provides.

The nutritional estimate listed here is mostly based on the scrambled tofu. The toppings aren't part of it.

Nutritional Facts

- o Fat – 13.1g
- o Saturated Fat – 2.3g
- o Carbohydrates – 3.8g
- o Protein – 20.3g
- o Fiber – 0.9g
- o Sugar – 1.2g
- o Sodium – 486mg
- o Calories – 206
- o Serving Size – one person

Lunch

Avocado Salad

This meal is the perfect blend of high-fat, low-carb, and moderate protein, keto vegan meal. It gets its good fatty acids from the avocado, olive oil, and grass-fed cheese. Make sure that you only use the grass-fed kind of cheese because it contains tons of anti-inflammatory omega-3 acids and CLA; plus the other types tend to promote inflammations and are high in omega-6 but low in the different areas.

The salad is chock full of antioxidants and phytonutrients. The red onions contain quercetin and anthocyanins, which protects brain tissue and reduce oxidative stress all through the body.

The various herbs and fresh lemon help in improving digestion since they contain enzymes and citric acid that improves the digestive process.

The salad doesn't take long to prepare. And it keeps you feeling full and satisfied for several hours in the day.

Ingredients

- Baby spinach or spring mix (1-2 handfuls)
- Small bunch of kale
- Diced red onion (1/4)
- Chopped up celery (2-4 stalks)
- One avocado (sliced into chunks)
- Squeezed lemon (1/2)
- Grass-fed cheese cut into chunks (four ounces)
- Two ounces of olive oil
- Ground ginger (or shredded)
- Chopped red and yellow bell pepper (1/2)
- Herbs like oregano, thyme, and basil (for taste and aroma)

Preparations

Get all your ingredients ready. Chop the ones that need chopping, and then add all of them into a salad bowl and toss it to give it a beautiful appearance. Squeeze your lemon over the salad, and apply the olive oil and herbs to the top. Serve the salad into little bowls and enjoy.

Nutrition Facts

- Total Fat (47g) – 72%
- Protein (17g) – 34%
- Total Carbs (26g) – 9%
- Calories – 569
- Dietary Fiber (13g) – 52%
- Serving size - 1 salad

Shirataki Noodles with Almond Butter Sauce

These Japanese noodles are often dubbed 'zero' or 'miracle' noodles because they contain no carbs or calories. They're made from the konjac yam (elephant yam). You can either buy them from health-food stores or order from online.

Ingredients

- One pack of Shirataki noodles
- Shredded cabbage (1/4)
- Almond butter (one tablespoon)
- One small carrot (cut into tiny batons)
- Cloves garlic (minced)
- Three spring onions (diced)
- Long-stem broccoli (100g)
- Coconut or mild olive oil (one tablespoon)
- 1-2 teaspoons of sriracha sauce (depends on how spicy you want it)
- Two tablespoons of coconut aminos
- Soy or tamari sauce (optional)

Preparation

Heat the olive oil in a large saucepan – using a medium flame, and add the onions and garlic. Cook them for a few minutes until they become soft, and then add the remaining vegetables.

Get your shirataki noodles ready by emptying them from the packet and rinsing with warm water. Once you're done, add them in with the vegetables in the saucepan.

When the meal is almost cooked, add the sriracha, almond butter, and coconut aminos to the pot and stir into the contents to create a warm sauce. Allow it to cool a bit before serving into small bowls.

Nutrition Contents

Based on the serving amount:

- o Protein – 8.1g
- o Fiber – 7.9g
- o Calories – 190
- o Carbs – 19.3g

Vegan Thai Soup

Ingredients

- Sliced mushrooms (three)
- Julienned red onion (1/2)
- Two cloves of garlic (chopped)
- Julienned red bell pepper (1/2)
- 500ml of vegetable broth or water (two cups)
- Thai chili (1/2)
- Ten ounces of cubed tofu (275g)
- Soy or tamari sauce (one tablespoon)
- Lime juice (half lime)
- Freshly chopped cilantro (a handful)
- Canned coconut milk (400ml)
- Brown, cane, or coconut sugar (one tablespoon)
- Finely chopped ginger root (1/2 inch piece)

Preparation

Place all your vegetables, the coconut milk, vegetable broth (or water), and sugar in a large pot. Start boiling the contents of the pan over medium heat for about five minutes. After the time is up, add the tofu and continue cooking for another five minutes or more.

Turn off the heat. Add the fresh cilantro, tamari, and lime juice to the pot and stir. You could store the soup in a sealed container in the refrigerator for about five days or in the freezer for more.

Side Tips

Feel free to use any sweeteners or vegetables you want if these ones don't work for you. If you're not a fan of spicy foods you can always remove the chili and add any other type that you like – some spicy sauce even.

You can also replace the tamari or soy sauce with sea salt. Use parley or any other fresh herb if you don't like cilantro; or omit the ingredient altogether.

Nutrition Contents

- o Fat – 27.6g
- o saturated fat – 19.7g
- o protein – 14.8g
- o carbohydrates – 15.6g
- o fiber – 3.2g
- o sugar – 5.3g
- o sodium – 297.4 mg
- o calories – 339
- o Serving size – ¼ of the recipe

Dinner

Zucchini Lasagna

Ingredients

For the Vegan Ricotta:

- Nutritional yeast (two tablespoons)
- Dried oregano (two teaspoons)
- Fresh basil (1/2 cup, finely chopped)
- Sea salt (one teaspoon) and a pinch of black pepper

- The juice of one medium lemon (30ml)
- Extra virgin oil (one tablespoon)
- ½ cup of water (more or less is required depending on if you're tofu)
- Vegan parmesan cheese (1/4 cup)
- Three cups of raw macadamia nuts or blanched almonds (you could also use $1^1/_6$ ounces of extra-firm block tofu instead)

The Rest

- Three medium zucchini squash or eggplant substitute (thinly sliced with a mandolin)
- Marinara sauce (28-ounce jar)

Preparation

Before beginning, preheat your oven to 375⁰F or 176⁰C. Get a blender or food processor and add the macadamia nuts to it and blend until the contents become a fine meal. Add the remaining ingredients (fresh basil, yeast, lemon juice, salt, pepper, olive oil, vegan parmesan cheese (optional) and water) to the blended macadamia nuts. Make sure everything assumes a well- puréed mixture or paste.

Taste your mixture to find out if there's any need to adjust the seasonings. You could add more pepper and salt for flavor, yeast for more cheesiness, and the lemon juice to brighten things up.

Pour a cup of the marinara sauce into your baking dish (9x13 inches or similar size) and line the sides with the thinly cut zucchini. Scoop small amounts (spoonful) of the ricotta mixture over your zucchini; spreading it to form a thin layer over the dish.

Add another layer of marinara sauce; topping it with more slices of zucchini. Continue this process until you exhaust all your fillings. Make sure that the top two layers are made up of the zucchini and sauce. Once that's done, sprinkle the vegan parmesan cheese on top of the dish and then cover it using the tin foil.

Bake the lasagna for around 45 minutes before removing the foil and baking again for over 15 minutes. You'll know when it's ready when your zucchini is pierced easily with a knife. Allow the dish to cool for about 10-15 minutes before you begin serving.

Store the leftovers in the refrigerator for around 2-3 days or a month in the freezer.

Side Note

The nutritional information is roughly estimated without adding the olive oil or parmesan cheese.

Nutritional Content

- Fat – 34g
- Saturated fat – 5.4g
- Sodium – 495mg
- Carbohydrates – 10g
- Fiber – 5g
- Sugar – 4.5g
- Protein – 4.7g
- Calories – 338
- Serving – 1 to 9 squares

Vegan Keto Walnut Chili

Ingredients

- Five Stalks of celery (finely diced)
- Two Cloves of garlic (minced)
- Chili powder (two teaspoons)
- Ground cumin (four teaspoons)
- Diced zucchini (two)
- Three cups of water
- Coconut milk (1/2 cup)
- Cremini mushrooms (eight ounces)
- Ground cinnamon ($1^1/_2$ teaspoons)
- Extra virgin olive oil (two tablespoons)
- Smoked paprika ($1^1/_2$ teaspoons)
- Two finely diced green bell peppers
- Tomato paste ($1^1/_2$ tablespoon)
- Diced tomatoes (one 15-ounce can)
- Salt and pepper
- Raw walnuts minced (one cup)
- Crumbled soy meat ($2^1/_2$ cups)
- Unsweetened cocoa powder (one tablespoon)
- Fresh cilantro leaves (two tablespoons)

Serve the chili with sliced avocados and radishes (two tablespoons)

Preparations

Add your oil to a large pot and heat it over a medium flame. Add the celery and boil for around 4 minutes. After that, add the chili powder, garlic, cinnamon, paprika, and cumin to the pot and keep stirring until you get the fragrant aroma.

Add the mushrooms, zucchini, and bell peppers, and leave to cook for another 5 minutes. Once the time elapses, put in the chipotle, fresh tomatoes, coconut milk, tomato paste, soy meat, cocoa powder, and walnuts. Lower the flame to medium to low and allow the broth to simmer for around 20-25 minutes or until it becomes thick and the veggies turn soft.

Use the pepper and salt to spice up the chili, and then use your avocado, cilantro, and radishes as toppings.

Vegetable Noodles with Smoked Tofu and Peanut Sauce

This noodle dish is both stunning and colorful with a delicious side of peanut sauce that's rich in healthy fats. The smoked tofu serves as a delicious alternative to meat. And it has a richness that tons of people appreciate when they make the switch to the vegan diet.

Ingredients

- Thinly sliced smoked tofu (200g)
- Three spring onion scallions (sliced into thin rounds)
- A half large cucumber
- A handful of cashews
- Peeled mouli daikon (one)
- Two courgettes zucchini
- Black sesame seeds (one tablespoon)
- One large beetroot (peeled)
- A handful of fresh coriander cilantro leaves
- Small sesame oil for frying
- Lime wedges (for serving)

For the peanut sauce

- Smooth peanut butter (three full tablespoons)
- One finely diced red chili (deseeded)
- Two large cloves of garlic (sliced or minced)
- Soy sauce (one tablespoon)
- Small ginger (peeled and diced)
- The juice from half a lime
- Sriracha (one tablespoon)

Preparations

Use a spaghetti blade to spiralize your mouli, courgettes, and beetroot. Do the same for the cucumber; this time around using a ribbon blade. Once you're

133

done, arrange your vegetable noodles in a bowl.

Heat a frying pan with a splash of sesame oil and fry the smoked tofu. When it's ready, remove the tofu and set it aside. Use the same pan to dry-fry the cashews for a few minutes, and then chop them up roughly.

When you're done with the cashews, add a tiny splash of oil to the pan and fry the chili, ginger, and garlic over low heat for a couple of minutes. Add the peanut butter and a reasonable amount of water to even out the broth to become a smooth sauce.

Turn off the flames and whisk in the lime juice, soy sauce, and sriracha into the pan before transferring the contents to a bowl.

Sprinkle the spring onions, cashews, and coriander leaves over the noodles and place the tofu around the dish. Add the sesame seeds and serve the meal with the hot sauce as a side dish.

As soon as you mix the sauce with the noodles, the vegetables will soften a bit and absorb the flavors of the dressing. You can serve the dish with extra lime wedges on the side.

Snacks Options

Sometimes, you just need a light snack to put you in the mood for the day. While you can't have a bag of chips or doughnuts, there are several keto-vegan alternatives that are just as satisfying and serve as a healthier option.

Whatever your reason for wanting a snack, there's no shame in letting go once in a while, as long as it's with a sensible option.

Let's take a look at some of the healthy snack options;

Keto Vegan Low-Carb Crackers

This crackers recipe allows you to satisfy your cravings and taste buds without feeling guilty over the process.

Ingredients

- Almond flour (one cup)
- Sunflower seeds (two tablespoons)
- Flax meal or whole psyllium husks (one tablespoon)
- Coconut oil (one tablespoon)
- Water (two tablespoons)
- Salt (3/4 teaspoon)

Preparation

Heat up your oven to about 350°F. Get a food processor and blend the sunflower seeds, almond flour, psyllium, and sea salt together; then pulse in water and coconut oil until dough forms.

Extract the dough ball on a sheet or parchment paper and flatten it. Cover the batter with another paper and roll it to about 1/8 to 1/6 inches.

Place the dough on a cutting board and remove the parchment paper. Use a knife or pizza cutter to cut into tiny squares (1-inch). After you're done the cutting, sprinkle the Sea Salts on the surface to add a little flavoring (optional).

Place the cut square dough on a baking sheet and place inside the oven. Leave to bake less than 350°F until the edges start turning brown and crisp (within 5 minutes).

crackers to cool on the rack before separating into squares. They at room temperature covered in a dish in the refrigerator. If you acker, try sprinkling the sea salt on the top of the dough before you start baking it.

Nutrition Facts	
Best Keto Low Carb Crackers (Almond Flour, Paleo)	
Amount Per Serving (0.5 cup)	
Calories 151	Calories from Fat 117
	% Daily Value*
Total Fat 13g	20%
Saturated Fat 2g	10%
Cholesterol 0mg	0%
Sodium 291mg	12%
Potassium 21mg	1%
Total Carbohydrates 6g	2%
Dietary Fiber 3g	12%
Sugars 0g	
Protein 4g	8%
Calcium	4.7%
Iron	4.9%
* Percent Daily Values are based on a 2000 calorie diet.	

Additional Info	
Net Carbs	3g
% Carbs:	8.3%
% Protein:	11%
% Fat:	80.7%

Keto Energy Balls (No Bake)

You only need three ingredients for this easy-to-make snack recipe.

- Coconut flour (3/4 cup)
- Tahini (2 cups)
- And a sticky sweetener (your choice)

Coconut flour is needed for this recipe since it helps in providing a durable and cake-like texture. But if it doesn't work for you, it can be easily substituted with oat flour.

Monk fruit maple syrup is the best option to use here for your sweetener. It has pretty much the same consistency of the other sweeteners, except it contains low levels of carbs and sugar.

Preparation

Get a large mixing bowl and add your tahini to it. Make sure that it's smooth and mixable. Heat up in a microwave or stove if it's firm or stiff.

After that, add your syrup and mix well. Shortly afterward, add the coconut flour to the mixture and stir thoroughly until everything is fully incorporated. Continue adding more flour to the batter if it's too thin until you achieve the desired thickness.

Use parchment paper or foil to line a clean plate, and then use your hands to roll the dough into small balls. Place the rolled balls on the plate and refrigerate them until they become firm.

The low-carb keto energy balls can be stored up to two weeks in a refrigerator, or five months in a freezer.

Nutrition Content

- o Calories – 57kcal
- o Carbohydrates – 3g
- o Protein – 2g
- o Fat – 4g
- o Fiber – 1.5g
- o Vitamin A – 3%
- o Vitamin C – 1%
- o Iron – 2%
- o Calcium – 2%

Fluffy Crispy Keto Waffles (Vegan Option)

Ingredients

- Baking powder (1/4 teaspoon)
- Ground flaxseed (one tablespoon)
- Non-dairy milk (1/2 cup)

- Vanilla extract (1/4 teaspoon)
- Granulated sweetener (one tablespoon, optional)
- Vanilla, brown rice protein powder 17g (1/2 scoop)
- Oat or wheat flour (1/4 cup)

Preparations

Add all your dry ingredients in a mixing bowl and set aside. Get another bowl and add your baking powder, flaxseed, vanilla extract, and a ¼ cup of the non-dairy milk together; whisk everything and allow to sit for at least 5 minutes so it can begin gelling up.

Turn on your waffle iron and allow to heat up for a while. Combine the contents of the two different bowls and add the extra milk to them until it forms a thick batter. Cook on the waffle iron for several minutes until you use up all the batter

Heat up the waffle iron and while it's heating up, combine the two bowls and add the extra 1/4 cup of milk until a thick batter is formed. Cook on the waffle iron until all the dough is used up.

If you want your waffles to be crispier, toast them in a toaster as soon as you're done cooking them. You could also store the waffles in a freezer to enjoy much later; wrap them in a parchment paper and put inside a Ziplock bag. Place them in the toaster if you want to reheat the frozen waffles.

Nutritional Content

- o Fat – 5g
- o Fiber – 10g
- o Protein – 20g
- o Calories – 162kcal
- o Carbohydrates – 15g
- o Vitamin A – 5%
- o Vitamin C – 3%
- o Calcium – 4%
- o Iron – 5%
- o Serving – one

Chapter Fourteen

Dessert Recipes

It might seem intimidating to create keto-vegan desserts since most of the fun ones require eggs and milk. It's tricky, but certainly not impossible. You just need to be creative with your ideas or seek outside help for recipes to use.

There are tons of ideas to borrow from; just check from a few of the recipes listed here.

Peanut Butter Nutella Cookies (Flourless)

This cookie is perfect for people who don't feel like choosing between using only peanut butter or Nutella. The two yummy treats are combined into one mouthwatering delicacy. You don't need much to make these flourless cookies – just three ingredients. And it doesn't take long to make – less than fifteen minutes.

Ingredients

- One cup of homemade Nutella
- Two egg substitutes (flax eggs)
- Cashew or almond butter (One cup)
- Two cups of coconut palm sugar (granulated)

Preparations

Begin by preheating the oven to about 350⁰ and then line a large-sized cookie sheet using greaseproof paper. Once you're done with that, set it aside.

Bring out two bowls mixing bowls and use the first one to mix the Nutella, one cup of ground coconut palm sugar, and one of the flax eggs until everything blends completely. Do the same for the second bowl with peanut butter.

Scoop small balls (about two inches) of each dough (the Nutella and peanut butter) and press them lightly together before placing them on the cookie sheet. As soon as you're done setting out the cookies, press each one of them down with a fork; then bake in the oven for about 10-12 minutes or until it assumes a lightly golden-brownish color. Make sure that it's still soft even with the change in color.

After that, take out the cookies from the oven and allow them to cool down on the sheet for at least 10 minutes before transferring them to another place to continue cooling. You can store the cookies for up to a week provided it's kept at room temperature, or for two months when frozen.

Keto Gingerbread Cookies (Nut and Gluten-Free)

Thankfully there are vegan alternatives for milk and eggs which make enjoying your favorite gingerbread cookie possible while following the keto-vegan diet. This cookie doesn't require baking.

But before we get into that, let's consider the frosting options used in glazing the top of the cookies. There's the option of making it yourself from scratch or sticking with the store-bought frostings.

Homemade Dairy-Free Cream Cheese Frosting

The process is relatively easy seeing as you only need like five ingredients;

- Soaked unsalted cashews (four cups)
- Lemon juice (1/2 cup)
- Coconut oil (1/4 cup)
- Water (1/3 cup)
- Liquid stevia or any other sweetener of your choice

Pour out the water from the soaked cashews. With the aid of a high-speed blender, get all five of your ingredients and blend them until they acquire a thick and creamy texture. Taste the mixture to make sure it's sweet enough for what you have in mind. And if it isn't, add more stevia. Transfer the mixture into an airtight container and place in the refrigerator; allowing it to thicken considerably.

But if you decide to go with the store-bought option, you could still spice things up with a few tricks here. Allow the cream cheese to become soft at room temperature, and then mix it with your sweetener and cinnamon until you get the texture of your desire.

If you want your frosting to be 100% sugar-free, you could always use pure maple syrup and agave nectar to get the right kind of sweetness.

Making the Gingerbread Cookie

You could use sunflower seed butter (with no sugar) as your choice spread. Frost the butter with your sweetened store-bought cream cheese.

Ingredients

- Coconut flour (3/4 cups)
- Nutmeg (one tablespoon)

- Ground ginger (two tablespoons)
- Two cups of cashew butter (or any nut or seed butter)
- Cinnamon (one tablespoon)
- Sticky sweetener (1/2 cup)
- Cream cheese frosting (one serving)

Preparation

Add your sticky sweetener to your cashew butter in a microwave bowl and allow it to melt. Then add the dry ingredients to the container and mix the contents very well until it forms a thick batter. You could always put more coconut flour to the mixture if the dough is too thin; if it's too thick, try adding more water to reduce the thickness.

Line your baking pan with parchment paper. Transfer the batter to its surface and press firmly in place. Once that's done, refrigerate the dough.

After the cookies are strong enough, get your frosting and coat the top with it, and then refrigerate again for about thirty minutes to make it get slightly firmer.

When the cookie is ready, cut the batter into bars and enjoy the delicacy. If you used the homemade cream and cheese frosting, you could store the gingerbread cookie for up to two weeks in the refrigerator.

Nutrition Contents

- Calories – 196kcal
- Fat – 16g
- Protein – 7g
- Fiber – 7g
- Carbs – 10g
- Calcium (1%)
- Vitamin A – 1%
- Vitamin C – 2%
- Iron - 2%
- Serving – 1Bar

Zucchini Brownies (Flourless)

You can use any of the several types of chocolate to ensure that your brownies are healthy and free of refined sugar.

- ❖ **Stevia Sweetened Chocolate Chips** – these ones don't have any bitter aftertaste melt pretty well. They're ketogenic and low-carb chocolate ship options.
- ❖ **Baking chocolate (100%)** – it's pure cocoa with zero sweetness.
- ❖ **Dairy-free vegan chocolate chips** – they're suitable for individuals on the Paleo and vegan diets.

As long as chocolate isn't an issue for you, any of the baking chocolates should work for you although you might want to consider sticking with the darker varieties since you're already getting sweetness from your sweetener of choice.

Ingredients

- 1/2 cup of applesauce (replacing eggs)
- Cocoa powder (two tablespoons)
- Coconut oil (1/3 cup)
- Granulated sweetener (3/4 cup) or coconut palm sugar
- Arrowroot powder (three tablespoons) or corn starch as a substitute
- Grated zucchini with moisture removed (1/4 cup)
- 225g Chocolate chips of choice ($1^1/_4$ cups)

Preparation

Heat up the oven to about 350^{0}F. Line a small pan (8 x 8 inches) with tin foil or parchment paper. Grease it up a little bit and then set it aside.

Combine your coconut oil and chocolate in a microwave-safe bowl and melt them until the texture is smooth. Transfer the batter to a larger bowl where you'll add your applesauce, zucchini, and granulated sweetener. Mix everything properly. Add the cocoa and arrowroot powder and whisk the batter until everything is smooth and combined.

Pour the mixture into the pan lined with tin foil, and spread it out evenly. Place into the oven and bake for around 20-25 minutes, or until a toothpick stuck in the center comes out 'clean.'

When it's ready, remove from the oven/microwave and allow the brownies to cool in the pan for a few minutes (fifteen or more) before you move it to a wire rack to cool down completely.

Side Note

You could decide to use flax eggs as your substitute if you can't get applesauce. They work just as well, even though the eggs have a very oily exterior. Banana also works too, but it has a slightly overpowering taste; which is why we chose the applesauce in the first place because it's perfectly balanced.

To get the best texture, it's advisable to keep your zucchini brownies refrigerated. They could also be stored in the freezer too.

If you love that ultra-gooey fudgy brownie feel, try under-baking them and leaving to cool overnight in the fridge before cutting them into smaller bar shapes.

Nutrition Content

- o Fat – 13g
- o Calories – 151 kcal
- o Carbohydrates – 5g
- o Protein – 5g
- o Fiber – 3g
- o Vitamin A – 2%
- o Vitamin C – 1%
- o Calcium – 2%
- o Iron - 2%
- o Serving: 1 brownie

Extra Tips

Lining your pan with tin foil or parchment paper makes it easy to remove the brownies when they're ready. It also bakes them more evenly.

Before you start adding your other ingredients, melt your chocolate chips and coconut oil first, as it ensures that the coconut oil doesn't separate when you're in the middle of baking. You could always use a small pan if you want to get thicker brownies.

Banana Bread (without Flour and Oats)

This healthy cake bread is both fluffy and light on the inside, filled with great banana flavors, and tender on the outside. This banana bread can be enjoyed as a light breakfast, healthy snack, or even dessert – it's multipurpose.

Unlike the customary banana cakes, this keto-vegan-friendly version doesn't require butter, flour, oil, or sugar. But somehow, you'll find it difficult to tell the difference between the traditional one and our version.

Since it's free from gluten, sugar, and dairy products, this recipe works for most dietary lifestyles.

Ingredients

- Cinnamon (one teaspoon)
- Baking powder (one teaspoon)
- Blanched almond flour (two cups)
- Coconut oil (half cup)
- Two flax eggs
- Salt (1/4 teaspoon)
- Vanilla extract (one teaspoon)
- Two large overripe bananas (mashed)
- Granulated sweetener (two tablespoons) although it's optional

Preparation

Preheat your oven to around 350°F and apply grease to a baking pan (10 x 10 inches should work). Set it aside once you're done greasing. Combine of all the dry ingredients in a big mixing bowl and ensure that they blend well.

Get a different bowl and melt your coconut oil. Mash your bananas (if you haven't already done so) and whisk them together with the flax eggs. Combine the wet and dry mixtures into one bowl and blend until everything incorporates fully.

Once you're satisfied with your results, pour the batter into your greased-lined pan. Bake the dough for about 40-50 minutes or until your toothpick comes out clean when you stick it in the center of the cake. When it's ready, allow cooling in the pan for at least 10 minutes before moving it to a wire rack to get cold. Cut the bread into desired slices and enjoy.

You could also store the banana bread in the refrigerator or freezer for up to three days.

Nutritional Content

- o Carbohydrates – 8g
- o Fat – 8g
- o Protein – 12g
- o Calories – 142kcal
- o Vitamin A – 4%
- o Calcium – 2%
- o Vitamin C – 3%
- o Fiber – 4g
- o Iron – 4%
- o Serving – 1 slice per person

Healthy Blueberry Breakfast Cake (Flourless)

While this cake is pretty much delicious on its own, it tastes a lot better when a thick layer of frosting is added to it.

Now for the cream cheese frosting;

Combine all your ingredients in a high-speed blender and allow it to mix until a smooth batter is all that remains. Use the instructions below to figure out what you need to prepare the frosting.

Select one package of dairy-free or full-fat cream cheese of your choice (250g/8 ounces). Get a large mixing bowl and add three tablespoons of sticky sweetener and a ½ teaspoon of cinnamon to your softened cheese.

Mix the combination very well until it's smooth. And if the mixture turns out to be too thick, you could slowly add water or milk to make it creamier. Once you're done baking the blueberry cake, you can spread the frosting over it.

Low-Carb Protein Frosting

Mix 1-2 scoops of vanilla protein powder with a ¼ cup of your granulated sweetener of choice, and ½ teaspoon of cinnamon in a mixing bowl and steer well.

Add a cup of yogurt (coconut or any other type) and a ¼ teaspoon of the vanilla extract and blend together in the bowl. Make sure the batter is really thick so that the frosting would hold well. And once your cake has cooled down, spread the frosting on top of it.

Cake Ingredients

- Two cups of rolled oats (gluten-free) ground into flour
- A pinch of sea salt
- Baking powder (one tablespoon)
- A cup of Almond Milk (or any one you prefer)
- Vanilla extract (one teaspoon)
- One flax egg

- Coconut palm sugar or any other ground sweetener of your choosing (1/2 cup)
- Almond butter (seed butter)
- Blueberries (1/2 to 1/4 cup)

Preparation

Heat the oven to around 350⁰F and line your baking pan with parchment paper or foil, then set it aside. Add all your dry ingredients in a large bowl and mix them properly.

Get another bowl and whisk your eggs in them, then add the unsweetened applesauce, melted coconut oil, and sticky sweetener (coconut palm sugar) and mix well.

Combine both your dry and wet ingredients in one bowl and blend well. Once you're through, fold your blueberries. Pour the batter in your baking pan and bake for around 35-40 minutes. When it's ready, allow the cake to cool for a little bit inside the pan before transferring it to your wire rack for more cooling.

As soon as your blueberry cake is cold enough, add the frosting to the top before cutting into slices and serving. You can also store it in a refrigerator for as much as five days or in a freezer for a month or two.

Nutritional Content

- o Fat – 11g
- o Protein – 8g
- o Calories – 135kcal
- o Carbohydrates – 7g
- o Fiber – 4g
- o Vitamin A – 4%
- o Vitamin C – 3%
- o Iron – 4%
- o Calcium – 2%
- o Serving – one slice

Conclusion

Embarking on any diet is never easy. There are several kinds of difficulties and challenges to navigate. That's where guides like these come in handy – to smoothen the process. It's designed to help you on your journey towards a healthy and happier lifestyle.

The ketogenic vegan diet is different from all the other fad diets in many ways. One, it resets your entire system and how it stores and deals with excess fat. It's like hitting the reset button and starting all over again on a journey.

There are tons of benefits associated with the diet (which we covered in here), some of which include fewer health problems and longevity. Another one has to do with sustained energy that's better than what the glucose stores did back then. And just as there are tons of positive sides to the diet, there are also a few issues and difficulties that put people off the process entirely.

Determining the right fat concentration to consume daily could be tricky sometimes, especially without help. While it's possible just to empty a bottle of olive oil in your mouth all day – and for the rest of your diet period, it's quite boring and tedious. Not to mention, the method is far from suitable. You need to take the time to work out the net carb ratio that works for your weight class before proceeding.

On its own, the vegan diet is already quite challenging. Adding the ketosis to the mix takes it to a whole new level. But in the end, the rewards are numerous. You just have to be patient enough to see it through.

If at first, you can't achieve ketosis, don't fret too much. Give it time and allow your body to work the kinks out; no matter how long it takes. Following a plant-based ketogenic diet is all about listening to your body and what it needs at a certain point. Don't be afraid to do what feels right to you, regardless of whether it's similar to what other dieters do to get results.

Everyone's body works differently from the next person. Remember that the next time you start comparing your progress levels to that of your colleague or friend. Focus more on enjoying the ride and less on the outcome. You need to work at getting everything you want since no one is going to hand you the perfect body and lifestyle on a platter.

Whatever you do, remember not to push yourself too hard, or it could compromise everything you worked to achieve.

28936981R00093

Printed in Great Britain
by Amazon